Creepy Dudes An Anthology of True Crime

Sarah Powe

Published by Trellis Publishing, 2021.

While every precaution has been taken in the preparation of this book, the publisher assumes no responsibility for errors or omissions, or for damages resulting from the use of the information contained herein.

CREEPY DUDES AN ANTHOLOGY OF TRUE CRIME

CREEPY DUDES

SARAH POWE

Mark Twitchell

"I was tentative about reaching out because I thought I couldn't offer much and doubted anyone could look past my reputation to the see the human being. But trying is definitely worthwhile if it means finding just one meaningful, mutually fulfilling friendship. My crime doesn't define who I am or represent me at all. I've made some terrible, regrettable choices in the past and I've come to terms with the consequences. Now I seek to infuse purpose into my life. Connection is a huge part of that. My creative engine never slows, so I produce artwork constantly and craft novels or screenplays to manifest my relentless imagination. I'm insightful, passionate and philosophical with a great sense of humor. I enjoy tennis, chess and clever story telling. I love the rain and the music of artists like Sia, Jackie Evancho and Arcade Fire. I'm looking for an interesting, intelligent, open-minded, delightfully imperfect woman to relate to and share amusing observations with...as well as potentially a long weekend every few months if it gets there naturally."[1]

Online dating has become the norm for many of us. Busy lives, children, sometimes working two jobs in order to provide as a single parent, means that it's not so easy anymore to meet people in 'real life'. But this profile is different – this profile belongs to prisoner Mark Twitchell, a convicted murderer who used one of the most popular dating sites around, *PlentyofFish.com*, to lure his victims to an empty garage, where he hoped to satisfy his lust for blood. His first attempt went wrong, and his victim got away – the next was not so lucky.

Mark

Not a lot is known about Mark Twitchell's childhood. He was born on July 4th, 1979, in Edmonton, Canada, to Norman and Mary Twitchell[2]

By all accounts, he had a normal, loving upbringing,[3]but life outside the family home was apparently significantly different and quite difficult for the boy.

Twitchell went to St Cecilia's Junior High, and then Archbishop O'Leary High School, where he was frequently teased and ostracised by his classmates and peers. His nickname was 'Twitch Hell', and the other kids would steal his glasses and taunt him with them, keeping them just out of reach in order to make Twitchell grab for them again and again.

One of his classmates recalled how he would feel unable to help Twitchell as the other kids bullied him.

"I felt really bad for the guy...I remember my dad taught him how to shoot a gun for the first time on a class trip - he could barely hold it after 10 shots. Now people think he's a killer. Unreal."[4]

He graduated from Archbishop O'Leary High School in 1997 and went on to study Radio and Television Arts at Northern Alberta Institute of Technology. He graduated in 2000, and married his first wife, Megan Casterella, on January 4th, 2001. The couple met in an online chat room. The young bride wanted to be close to her sister, so, after they married the young couple moved to Davenport, where Megan enrolled at Palmer College.

At first, Twitchell worked for American TV as a salesman in Davenport, before being transferred to Peoria, some 100 miles away. The couple moved so that Twitchell could be closer to work - however, he still spent much of his time in Davenport.[5]

The marriage lasted four years.

First Divorce

It was not only Megan who took her leave of Twitchell – after working with the company for two years, American TV 'released' him without revealing the reasons why.

The marriage had not been a happy one. When Megan filed for divorce in 2004, Peoria court documents showed that her husband had *"been found guilty of extreme and repeated mental cruelty."* That, plus the spiralling debt of $40,000, spelt the end of the marriage for Megan and Mark.

Although the marriage had been rocky and, by all accounts, abusive, their former landlord, Jody Kimbrell, said the couple had been model tenants – rent was never late, the unit was kept clean and tidy, and there were never any complaints from neighbors. Even after the pair divorced, and Twitchell moved out of the matrimonial home and into another unit in the complex, there was never any cause for concern.

Kimbrell even recalled that there was no friction after the divorce. *"They didn't really speak to each other, but they were cordial."*

Mark Twitchell was an avid Star Wars fan and used to buy and sell merchandise on the internet prior to his divorce.

"Star Wars dolls, paraphernalia, suits, outfits, he had it all – and he bought and sold them constantly...There was Stars Wars stuff all over the unit, but hey, whatever people collect, they collect."[6]

Twitchell's interest in Star Wars wasn't confined to the merchandise, however. Even after he moved to Peoria he remained a member of the 'Quad-Cities Jedi Order', a fan club dedicated to the films. He was also actively involved in Star Wars online forums and groups and was a prolific poster on the boards.

The Dark Side

Although Twitchell's obsessions seemed to be centered around the Sci-fi genre, his wife, Megan, caught glimpses of his more sinister side.

In a book written by investigative journalist Steve Lillebuen, Megan says *"He kind of had that really dark, secretive side...He would make comments like, 'You can't handle what goes on in my mind."*

That dark side stayed relatively hidden, apart from the few glimpses Megan caught, for quite some time. Twitchell's time on Star Wars forums had cemented his belief that he should make a fan film about the franchise, and he became more and more immersed in the fantasy, making costumes and spending time at Star Wars conventions.

It was during his marriage to Megan that Twitchell found a new way to have fun. Already well-versed on the internet through both his Star Wars forums and internet dating sites, Mark Twitchell started making up false profiles and tricking people into talking to him – a 'skill' which would eventually lead to something far darker.[7]

However, science fiction had a rival for Twitchell's attention, in the form of 'Dexter' – a TV show about Dexter Morgan, a blood-spatter analyst with Miami Police Department by day, and serial killer by night. Mark Twitchell had found his idol.

Jess

In the fall of 2005, Mark met Jess on the dating website, PlentyofFish.com, and in January 2007, Jess became the second Mrs Twitchell.[8] The honeymoon period came to an end that same year when Twitchell and a former girlfriend made contact on facebook.

Traci Higgins had met Mark Twitchell at the Northern Alberta Institute of Technology where they both studied, in 1997. Their friendship developed, and the pair became a couple. However, Twitchell's dishonesty caused problems in the relationship, and Traci broke it off. But in 2007 they found themselves back in touch – Traci, like Mark, had gone on to marry someone else, and again, like Mark, had gone through a divorce.

The fact that Twitchell had remarried did not deter the former girlfriend, and the pair met up for dinner, with the evening ending with 'a long kiss'. Contact continued between Mark and his mistress throughout 2008, and on October 10th of that year, the pair met up to go to the movies.

The movie, *Quarantine*, was not enough to hold their attention, and instead of watching the screen the couple 'made out' until it was finished, at around 5 pm, after which Traci went home alone. Twitchell, however, had other things on his mind,[9] something Traci would find out about later.

House of Cards

Mark Twitchell still saw himself as a big-time movie producer and harboured dreams of making it big in Hollywood. Towards the end of

September 2008, Twitchell gathered together a film crew, along with a few actors he had found through online casting-call agencies, and they all met at a converted garage he had rented and turned into a filming studio.

Twitchell, now into his third season of Dexter, had written a short film based on the show and called it *House of Cards*. Inspired by the character, Twitchell had turned the garage into his own 'kill room', complete with metal chair, and walls covered in plastic. The story centered on a writer who would lure other men by assuming a false identity on internet dating sites, pretending to be a woman. The killer would arrange to meet the 'dates' at home, where he would jump them, and bind the men with duct tape to the metal chair, which was bolted to the concrete floor. Before murdering the men, he would obtain their banking details and passwords, and once he had their information would brutally kill them and dismember their bodies before stuffing their body parts into plastic bags.

In the eight-minute movie, the killer bought time by using the passwords obtained before the killings to send emails and social media messages to the victims' friends and family, explaining their unexpected absences on a longer stay vacation.

The actor who played the part of the murderer, Robert Barnsley, flew in from Toronto on the promise of a $30,000 cheque for Twitchell's next movie, for his part in *House of Cards*.

The 20-year-old was more than a little surprised by the set-up when he arrived at the garage. The props were real – sharp knives, a stun gun, and a metal table. Although there had been mention of using real blood from a butcher, it was finally decided that they would use corn syrup and red food coloring.

Chris Heward was the actor playing the part of the victim. While he was duct taped to the chair, Barnsley was given a real sword and told to simulate sticking the sword into Heward's chest.

"I twisted the sword to the side, making it look like it was being twisted inside him. I would grind my teeth in the pleasure of killing him."

Heward found the experience unnerving. *"It was very uncomfortable...I was freaking out...I really didn't know these guys. At the time, I was thinking it was really dumb not to bring my agent or anybody with me."*

The final scene of the movie saw the killer sitting at a computer and closing down a fake woman's profile, before putting away a hockey mask – the same kind as had been worn during the murder. When his wife asked him how the story was coming along, the killer replied *"Really well, sweetie...It's true when they say the best way to succeed is to write what you know."*[10]

Lies

Earlier that year, in the Spring of 2008, Twitchell had found himself a job in sales. However, his obsession with his film-making took over and he stopped going to work, without telling Jess. By the time she found out, five months later, the marriage was already deeply in trouble. Their daughter had been born at the beginning of the year, and Jess was sleeping upstairs with the baby while Mark slept downstairs in the basement. He had set up a company called Xpress Entertainment, and was living off the investments backers had put into the company.

When Jess asked her husband what he was working on, in September 2008, he told her it was a film about a man who is having an affair. The premise of the story, he had told her, was that the man had arranged to meet a woman he had met online while telling his wife he was going to the gym. The woman is then attacked and murdered by a masked assailant. When Jess learned that the ending involved the woman being decapitated, she objected and asked her husband to change it.

Jess was quickly learning about her husband's darker side.

The couple, in a bid to solve their marital difficulties, were attending regular counselling sessions together, and Mark was seeing a psychiatrist by himself every Friday evening. On Friday, October 10th, Jess called her husband to ask where he had gone after his session. In a bizarre likeness to the script Jess had objected to, Mark told her he was at the gym. Jess, however, already knew that the gym they both used was closed, and told him so. He then claimed that he was at a different one.

Although the similarities to his story line were striking, there was one major difference. Although Twitchell had, indeed, spent the afternoon with a woman – his mistress Traci Higgins – he had a different kind of rendezvous planned for the evening.[11]

Gilles Tetreault

What nobody realized, however, was that Twitchell had already blurred the lines between fact and fiction. The filming at the end of September had clearly triggered something in his head, giving him the desire to feel what the killer felt.

The filming of the graphic murder scene had gone well, and everyone in the crew was happy with the results – everyone except Twitchell himself. It hadn't gone unnoticed by several members that the director had gone quiet towards the end of the shoot, and only seemed to cheer up when the crew decided that the remaining scenes were superfluous and that they should call it a wrap.[12] Was that when the seeds were finally sown in Twitchell's mind?

It could well have been, because, only a few days later, Twitchell came face to face with his first victim.

36-year-old Gilles Tetreault had been chatting to a woman named Sheena on the dating site, Plentyoffish.com, and she had asked him to meet her for a date. On October 3rd, 2008, Gilles arrived at the garage where Sheena had arranged to meet him. Although he felt it a little odd, he understood her concerns about not wanting to give her address out to a stranger. But when Tetreault entered the garage, there was no sign of the pretty blond woman he had arranged to meet. Instead, he was confronted by a masked man who attacked him with a stun baton, before pulling a gun on him and ordering him to lie down. As the assailant began to duct tape his victim's eyes closed, Tetreault was terrified.

"I started tearing up. A lot of things were going through my head. When they say your life flashes before your eyes, that's what it was. My family. They may never see me again."

Unsure of whether his attacker was going to rob him, rape him, or murder him, Tetreault decided to fight back with everything he had.

"I decided I'd better fight back. I'd rather die my way than his way."

As he began to fight, Gilles grabbed the gun, and, feeling the plastic, realized it wasn't a real firearm. That realization gave him strength, and he took hold of the first thing he could lay his hands on – a pair of handcuffs which had been lying on the floor.

As Tetreault fought for his life, his attacker began to rain punches down on him, but he managed to make it outside. His legs were shaking so much that he was unable to run, though, and he had only made it as far as the pathway when he felt himself being dragged back inside once more.

Tetreault knew that if he was taken back inside the garage again he would be dead, so, gathering all of his strength, the 36-year-old man fought back, again managing to break free from the man who was wearing what he could now see was a hockey mask.

Fortunately for Tetreault, a couple were walking by with their dog and stopped to see what was happening. As Tetreault pleaded with them to help him, the attacker, still wearing his hockey mask, told them everything was ok and that they were just fooling around. The couple left without helping, but it was enough to unnerve the assailant, and he turned and fled, leaving Tetreault to escape.[13]

Once home, Gilles decided to report the attack to the police and logged on to the internet to bring up 'Sheena's' profile as proof. However, the profile had already been deleted and now, Gilles realized, he had no proof of what had taken place, so he made the decision not to, for fear of not being believed.

Gilles Tetreault had had a lucky escape, but it wouldn't be long before he understood exactly how lucky he had been.

Johnny Altinger

Although Mark Twitchell had failed in his quest for murder, the incident with Gilles Tetreault had only strengthened his blood lust. He would try again, and this time he wouldn't fail.

On October 10th, 2008, only a week after his first attempt, Twitchell once again went online in search of his next victim. Plentyoffish.com yielded new prey, and Twitchell struck up a conversation with 38-year-old Johnny Altinger. This time, Twitchell portrayed himself as 'Jen' a 5'6" pretty brunette, who described herself as a hopeless romantic. She invited Johnny to meet up with her that evening, and naturally, he agreed.

Once again, directions to the garage were emailed. In his eagerness to meet Jen, Johnny arrived at the garage 45 minutes early, and, seeing the door open decided to go on in. Mark Twitchell was caught unawares – his kill room wasn't ready and he wasn't prepared when he heard Altinger call out Jen's name. As Johnny ducked under the plastic sheeting, he saw Twitchell, who told him that Jen had said she would be right back. Altinger knew something was terribly wrong, and made to leave, instructing Twitchell to tell Jen that he would come back later.

Twitchell was not going to let a second victim get away. After failing to kill Tetreault, Twitchell had changed his weapon of choice from the stun gun to a lead pipe, and as Altinger turned to leave Twitchell hit him over the back of the head with it, and carried on hitting, bringing it down onto Altinger's head over and over again.

Mark Twitchell had succeeded – Johnny Altinger was dead.

But the murderer wasn't finished. He had set up the garage to mirror the Kill Room in Dexter, complete with a metal table. It was on to this table that Twitchell dragged Johnny's lifeless body.

And it was there that he set about methodically dismembering him, relishing the feeling as he cut, sawed, and hacked his way through skin, muscle and bone, piece by piece.

Mark Twitchell finally had his taste of blood, in every sense. As he stood with his hands drenched in his victim's blood, he calmly ate a candy bar, before continuing with his gruesome task.

Of course, once the body was dismembered it had to be disposed of. Twitchell placed all of the body parts into plastic bags and put them in the trunk of his car. His first plan of action had been to drop them off the bridge into the river, but he changed his mind and instead threw them into a sewer.

His job was still not finished though. In order to deflect suspicion, Twitchell broke into Altinger's apartment and found his laptop. Altinger was still logged in, which made Twitchell's job so much easier, and he sat down in his victim's chair and sent emails to Johnny's friends, telling them he, 'Johnny', had run away to Costa Rica with a girl he had met, and that he would be gone for a couple of months.

He sent a further email to Johnny's workplace, telling his employer that he had resigned with immediate effect.

Twitchell stole the laptop – happy that he had covered his tracks.[14]

The Investigation

Unfortunately for Twitchell, the emails he had sent to Johnny's friends didn't convince them. This behavior was uncharacteristic for the man they knew.

They took the emails to the police, insisting that something had happened to their friend, but at first, the police weren't interested. After all, Johnny Altinger was a 38-year-old man and as such was free to come and go as he pleased. He had no history of mental illness, he wasn't considered a high-risk, and he lived alone, so for a few days, the police did nothing.

His friends would not give up, though, and eventually, the police agreed to investigate. The case made its way from desk to desk, and department to department, until it landed on the desk of Detective Bill Clark, a homicide detective, Clark was unimpressed – in a city with high crime he was a busy man, but nevertheless he decided to take a look, and attended a briefing about the case.

Johnny's friends had continued to receive emails from Johnny.

"I've met an extraordinary woman named Jen who has offered to take me on a nice long tropical vacation...We'll be staying in her winter home in Costa Rica, phone number to follow soon."

However, that phone number never arrived, and the only way Johnny's friends could contact him was via email, facebook, or MSN messenger. When they questioned why they couldn't reach him by phone they were told that the reception was bad.

It was lucky that Johnny had had the foresight to give the directions to the garage to a friend before he set off on his date. The police were able to track down the place and discovered that, rather than a woman named Jen, the house to which the garage belonged was rented by Mexicans, and that the tenant of the garage was a local filmmaker who was using the garage as some sort of studio.

The police interviewed Twitchell – he was cooperative and helpful and seemed genuinely bemused by the case. When the garage was searched, Twitchell was asked when he was last there, and he told officers that he hadn't been there since September. However, one of the officers noticed a lot of cleaning supplies on the table, along with a receipt. The receipt was dated October 15th. Twitchell played it down, claiming that he had forgotten that he had stopped by briefly to drop off some cleaning supplies, which he had forgotten about until then. Something didn't sit quite right. Detective Clark felt that it was too great a coincidence that a man had disappeared on a first date from the exact same place that was being used by a filmmaker. Twitchell was interviewed a second time.[15] The police decided to bring in crime scene investigators and asked Twitchell if he would give permission for them to go over the garage for evidence. He readily agreed, but then offered up some new information. He claimed that, on the night of Altinger's disappearance, he had been approached by a man who asked him to buy his red Mazda for $40. Officers followed Twitchell's directions and found the car about a mile away. The car was registered to Johnny Altinger, and police now had the connection between him and Twitchell.[16]

Apart from the Mazda, Clark found several more flaws in Twitchell's story, but he didn't have enough evidence to hold him, so he was released. Clark had read the scripts the crew had been working on, and had started to see similarities between the story and the disappearance. Although he didn't have enough to keep Twitchell there, Clark did have sufficient cause to seize Twitchell's car.

That was when his story began to unravel.

The Pontiac Grand Am was searched, and police found Twitchell's laptop, along with traces of blood, both in the trunk and on a knife which was next to the laptop. The computer was taken by technicians to see what could be found, and Clark was presented with a 42-page document which had been recovered from the deleted files, entitled 'The SK Confessions'. The first paragraph read: *"This story is based on true events. The names and events were altered slightly to protect the guilty. This is the story of my progression into becoming a serial killer."*

As Clark read on, he discovered that what the police had uncovered was a diary of the murder of Johnny Altinger. It detailed the dating ruse, the murder, and the intention of repeating a murder every Friday night. It also revealed the earlier attempted murder of Gilles Tetreault. However, the one detail Clark wanted more than any other was the whereabouts of Johnny Altinger's body – a detail which Twitchell had failed to record.[17]

Twitchell, still a free man, was put under 24-hour surveillance, with police concerned that he would kill again. On October 20th, 2008, ten days after Altinger's murder, they obtained a search warrant, and as they searched his house Jess took their daughter and left. She found her husband at his parents' house and told him the police suspected him of murder. She also questioned him about an incident which had happened recently, when she had caught Mark looking at a website which offered married people the chance to have affairs. At the time, Mark had told his wife that it was research for a freelance article, but when she confronted him again at his parents' house, Mark confessed. He had even been so devious as to hire an actor to play the part of an editor should Jess decide to check out her husband's story, a fact he admitted that day.

Jess left Mark there and then, and the next time she saw him was when she gave evidence at his trial.[18]

During the search of the couple's St. Albert home, they uncovered several pieces of incriminating evidence. A pair of Mark's recently washed jeans which still had traces of blood on them, and some blank postcards of Costa Rica – the place Johnny Altinger had supposedly gone with 'Jen'.

The search moved on to the garage, which the detectives now decided warranted a much closer look. Unlike Dexter, Twitchell hadn't managed to remove all traces of blood, and not only was there blood in the cracks on the table but they also found a large amount of blood spatter on the door, and less than two weeks later the blood from the garage, as well as the blood found in the trunk of Twitchell's car, was proven to be that of Johnny Altinger.

His Arrest

The police had all the evidence they needed, and on October 31st, 2008, Mark Twitchell was arrested for murder.

When Gilles Tetreault saw the news coverage, he realized that it was the same attacker, and came forward with his story. However, throughout all of their investigations, the police still had no idea where Johnny Altinger's body had been dumped. They brought Twitchell back to the garage in the hope that it would prompt him to reveal the location of his victim's remains, and on June 10th, 2009, he finally revealed where police could find the body by giving them a detailed map leading to the sewer where he had hidden the body parts.

The Trial

On March 16th, 2011, Mark Twitchell's murder trial began. He took the stand as the only witness for the defense, and told a story about how he had set Johnny Altinger up in an elaborate hoax to gain publicity for the movie. When Altinger realized this, according to Twitchell, he became irate and a fight ensued. A fight which led to Altinger's death. It was, Twitchell claimed, self-defense.[19]

A key piece of evidence in Twitchell's trial was the 42-page document, 'The SK Confessions'. He claimed that the initials 'SK' stood for his favorite author Stephen King – when in fact, it was believed that it stood for 'Serial Killer'. The jury heard the document read out loud, listening to graphic details of the killing, and the subsequent dismembering, of Johnny Altinger. There were some details which were held back, as they were thought to be too distressing for the members of the jury to hear. One such passage described how, when Twitchell cut off Altinger's head he played with it as if it was a puppet.

"I grabbed his jaw with my gloved hand and moved it while making a funny voice to make it look like it was talking, and chuckled to myself at the total silliness of it all."

Other details of the document, which Twitchell insisted were fictional, provided further insight into his psyche. He described the moment he cut open his victim's torso and watched the internal organs becoming displaced.

"If I had a sense of smell this might be disgusting for me. But I only find it fascinating...Most people fantasize and it only ever stays a fantasy. They don't have the disposition or the stomach to go all the way with their dark urges. But I do."

Talking of killing in a more general sense, Twitchell went on:

"I do not have any reservations about disposing of the negative people in this world who deserve a one-way ticket to the afterlife if such a thing exists."[20]

On April 12th, 2011, Mark Twitchell was found guilty of murder and sentenced to life in prison with no chance of parole for at least 25 years.

It was decided not to pursue the charge of the attempted murder of Gilles Tetreault, as it would not add to the maximum sentence he had already received.

Twitchell continued to cause controversy from inside Saskatchewan Penitentiary where he is serving his sentence, by buying a flat screen TV for his private cell, on which he was able to continue watching the show 'Dexter' – the same show which had inspired him to murder Altinger and attempt to murder Tetreault.[21]

As Bill Clark put *it "He's reliving his fantasy whenever he's watching that show...It's ridiculous to think that he would be allowed to do that. Maybe he's refining his skills?"*[22]

A worrying thought for everyone, but perhaps none more so than an ex-employer of Twitchell, who was mentioned in the 'SK Confessions', who was described as *"a twisted old fart who hated life and everything in it. I owed it to the world to remove him from its glorious surface and would take my chance when I was ready."*[23]

Internet Serial Killer

Thomas Griffin

Serial killers are a fascinating subject to the public. On one hand, we as a collective society are frightened by their horrific murders and indignant at how their heinous lives lasted for so long. On the other, we are fascinated by their complex lives and remarkable ingenuity—if anything, reading about them puts us temporarily in the mind of the killer themselves, simultaneously disgusted and a voyeur nonetheless. Maybe we just want to avoid situations for practical sakes where a trusting face may appear and help us recognize the signs of someone capable of these egregious crimes; other times, there's a voyeuristic *pleasure* that fuels our innate instincts.

This sentiment may not be more apropos for the serial killer **John Edward Robinson**. Known as the "Internet's first serial killer," he embodied a con man's savvy with reckless precision, taking at least eight women down his path until his conviction in 2003.

Early Life

It is the nature vs. nurture question: was this person born this way, or did their upbringing cause irrevocable harm and set them on the path of harming others. For John Edward Robinson, the analysis only offers more questions than it solves.

Born on December 27th, 1943, Robinson was reared into a middle-class suburban upbringing of Cicero, Illinois. The middle child of five children, with an alcoholic father employed in a blue-collar job as a machinist at Western Electric, and a strict, disciplinarian mother that pushed him towards success, his upbringing was relatively unremarkable. As a member of the Boy Scouts and later the Eagle Scouts, his troop even gave a variety show performance for England's Queen Elizabeth II. In 1957, he enrolled at Quigley Preparatory Seminary, a private school that trains young boys for priesthood, but he dropped out after a year for disciplinary issues.

By 1961, with priesthood not a fitting career, Robinson enrolled at Morton Junior College (also in Cicero) to train as a medical X-ray technician. He also married at the age of 21 to a woman named Nancy

Jo Lynch, so it seemed he was on his way towards attaining a normal life. He would drop out of Morton Junior College after two years, however, and move to Kansas City, MO.

It is at this point that we begin to see his "descent" into criminal behavior. Despite not having proper credentials, he managed to fake his way into a position at a prominent medical office. However, it wasn't just any medical office that he managed to become employed at; it was at Wallace Graham's office, the personal doctor of President Harry Truman. While those stakes may have been high to begin with, he had other plans in mind. All the while working surreptitiously, Robinson was embezzling funds for his own personal use by manipulating deposits and checks. Eventually, he was caught after embezzling nearly $33,000, sentenced to three years of probation and only found guilty of "stealing by means of deceit."

John Edward Robinson didn't stop there, however. Following his sentencing, he found employment at a television-rental store. Despite probation, he was found to be stealing merchandise and fired, but not brought up on criminal charges.

In 1970, he moved back to the Chicago area, unbeknownst to (or permitted by) his probation officer, gaining employment as an insurance salesman. By 1971, he was once again brought up on charges for embezzlement from the insurance agency that hired him and was subsequently ordered back to Missouri.

His sentencing was once again lenient, Robinson was given only an extended probation. In 1975, Robinson's probation was extended further yet after another arrest for securities and mail fraud related to a fake medical consultation business he formed in Kansas City.

Then, not declaring that he was on probation, he managed to find a systems analyst position at Mobil Oil Corporation. Remarkably, his probation officer even endorsed his new lifestyle by stating for the parole board that Robinson "does not appear to be an individual who is basically inclined towards criminal activities and is motivated towards achieving middle class values." In addition, another officer later stated that Robinson was "responding extremely well to probation supervision," and that she was "encouraging [Robinson] to advance as far as possible with Mobil Oil." Weeks after these glowing statements, Robinson was found to be stealing nearly 6,000 stamps from the company and was promptly fired.

"He did not work any type of legitimate job," Lt Rick Roth said. "Where he did not take steal the company for some kind of money."

If you're scratching your head at how this was permissible, remember that we're only covering some of the larger cons that he was involved with—in fact, his early track record is even more checkered the closer one looks into it—worse, we may never know the full extent of his prolific con man's life. While his story may seem to be a tamer version of "Catch Me If You Can"—Robinson was clearly an intelligent person—he demonstrates his ability to straddle the line between crime and appeasing society, cleverly blending his way in. For most people, these early convictions may have been crippling, but he clearly used deceit to achieve a place in society that would fuel his future crimes. Perhaps what is the most enraging is seeing how a clever person could evade authorities time and time again—weren't their mechanisms in place to prevent Robinson from committing the same crimes, time and time again? However, while he was "fooling" authorities, WORSE crimes were being committed using this same intelligence.

Beginning of the Murders

While he was committing the cons, John Edward Robinson was known ostensibly as a pillar of the community and a dedicated family man, now raising three children with his wife. Consistent with his days of youth, he became a Scoutmaster and a Sunday school teacher. Using his con man abilities to bolster himself in the community, he persuaded the board of directors of a local charitable organization by forging letter from the mayor of Kansas City (and other civic leaders) to their executive directors, commending his volunteering efforts and his status as a model citizen. He then orchestrated that he be placed as "Man of the Year" in 1979, throwing a festive awards luncheon in his own honor. Of course, this honor didn't go unchecked, especially as the Kansas Star reported on this event positively, and then retracted it when Robinson's track record of embezzlement came to light—tarnishing the reputation of a reporter and the newspaper's fact-checking mechanisms.

Of course, Robinson persevered, fooling those not familiar with anything more than the mask and image he was trying to present. With this facade in place, he used it as a front for his activities. He began to openly proposition the wives of his neighbors for sex, on one occasion causing a fist fight. Robinson also joined a secret sadomasochism cult called the International Council of Masters, becoming its "Slavemaster." The duties of the Slavemaster included luring victims to gatherings to be tortured and raped by cult members.

To serve these purposes and his own, he started more fraudulent shell companies named *Equi-Plus* and *Equi-2*. Nineteen-year old Paula Godfrey was the first victim of Robinson's plans, where he hired the unemployed and financially desperate woman to supposedly work as a sales representative. She, in turn, left for "training" under Robinson's wing, and then disappeared, her family uncertain of her whereabouts. Her family sent out a missing persons report. Robinson then typed up a letter in Godfrey's behalf, stating that she was doing fine and that she didn't want to see her family.

Godfrey remains "missing" to this day.

By 1985, Robinson met Lisa Stasi and her four-month-old daughter, Tiffany, at an abused women's shelter, offering her a promise of employment in Chicago. He offered her an apartment and daycare for her baby. It was an offer too good to refuse (or too good to be true). In turn, Robinson asked her to sign several sheets of blank stationery, as he convinced her that she would not have the time to do so as they would be traveling extensively. Simultaneously, Robinson contacted his brother and sister-in-law, unable to adopt a child through the traditional channels, and offered them a child whose mother had committed suicide. Charging them $5,500 in made-up fees, Robinson's brother and sister-in-law adopted Tiffany along with a set of forged adoption papers.

Lisa Stasi was never heard from again.

The Stasi family would receive a phone call from someone who a priest from the City Union Mission in downtown Kansas City. The priest called himself "Father Martin" and stated that he had seen Lisa and Tiffany, describing them as "doing fine" but they had left town with "a guy named Bill."

The family tried to verify the story, calling the mission back.

They are then told that there is no "Father Martin" at the mission.

Police would investigate, questioning Lisa's former husband who had a solid alibi. They also interviewed Robinson.

"He told me, yeah, she was referred to me," Detective Chuck Wilson recalled Robinson telling him. "I said I would put her up in my Kansas City outreach program. Lisa came to his office with a young man by the name of Bill who she said was her new boyfriend and that they were going to go off togethr and they were going to start a new life and she really thanked Robinson for all of his help and for being there to support her but she really thought things were coming together and she was really going to start a new life."

"Bill" and "Father Martin" were just names that Robinson used to throw the authorities off his trail.

Robinson's depravity didn't stop there. Twenty-seven year old Catherine Clampitt left her child with her parents in Wichita Falls, Texas in 1987. She moved to Kansas City to find employment and a better life for her family. Answering an ad placed by Robinson, she fell for the same trap as the previous women.

Clampitt would answer the ad that wanted an "executive secretary" who would work for a "busy CEO" named "John Dawson."

After answering the ad, Clampitt would vanish.

Clampitt's mother, however, would receive a typewritten letter purportedly from her daughter. The words do not sound like things her daughter would say. Her mother grew concerned and had Catherine's stepbrother call her workplace to speak with "John Dawson."

He is told that there is no "John Dawson" working there.

Clampitt's brother goes through her belongings and finds a hotel receipt signed by a John Robinson. Doing his own due diligence, he discovers that John Robinson owns the company that Clampitt went to work for, Equis II.

Clampitt's mother then goes to the company headquarters only to find out that the place has been closed down and that Robinson had been arrested earlier for fraud and theft.

"He was just a small-time con man," FBI agent Jeff Daniels said. "There was no indication that he had been involved in anything really much more than that."

Robinson benefited from the fact that all the detectives worked by hand and not via computers as they are now. Detectives were unable to make the connection between Godfrey, Stasi and Clampitt.

All three cases eventually go cold.

Clampitt's remains have not been found and her missing persons report remains open.

Incarceration and Next Phase

As most criminals (and especially serial killers) tend to, Robinson began to get careless. Between the years of 1987 to 1993, he was incarcerated in Kansas and Missouri for his multiple fraud convictions and parole variations. While this incarceration would be believed to reduce his criminal activities, it only increased his focus. At Western Missouri Correctional Facility, he managed to ingratiate himself to Beverly Bonner, the 49-year-old prison librarian. He must have been incredibly persuasive, as upon his release, Bonner left her husband and moved to Kansas to be employed by Robinson. This was all a set-up for Robinson's next plan, as he funneled Bonner's alimony checks to be forwarded to a Kansas P.O. Box. As a pattern from the previous women, her family never heard from her again. The checks kept arriving, being forwarded from Bonner's mother, and they were cashed—by Robinson, of course.

The Internet's Roleplay

Robinson was always on the lookout for the next scam to fuel is sadistic impulses. By his release in 1993, the Internet was readily available to the general public and a person of Robinson's intelligence was sure to take advantage of its wide reach. He roamed chat rooms and social networking sites, under the alias of his former sadomasochistic cult title, "Slavemaster," intent on finding women who were interested in submissive sexual roleplay amid the BDSM lifestyle (an acronym that blends "Bondage and Discipline" "Dominance and Submission" and "Sadism and Masochism" under one catchall).

The first victim he met online was forty-five year old Sheila Faith. Sheila had a 15-year-old daughter Debbie that was disabled, confined to a wheelchair due to spina bifida. Robinson managed to portray himself as wealthy and altruistic, offering to support both of them—offering Sheila a job and paying for Debbie's therapy. Sheila was convinced and moved from Fullerton, California to Kansas City.

Both mother and daughter immediately disappeared.

Faith's pension checks were dutifully cashed—by Robinson for the next seven years.

His crimes didn't stop there as the Internet only increased his reach. Robinson was beginning to develop a name for himself in the BDSM community, which not only was increasingly popular, but blurred the line between what actually qualified between consent and abuse.

By 1999, he found another victim, a 21-year-old Polish immigrant living in Indiana named Izabela Lewicka. She was an intellectual, often frequenting bookstores and being regarded as a regular patron by the staff of one bookseller in particular. Much like Sheila, he offered her employment and a bondage relationship, which she agreed to by filling out a 115-item "slave contract," giving Robinson carte blanche over nearly every aspect of her life, including her bank accounts and financial freedom.

To ensure her trust and to put up further smokescreens, Robinson bought her an engagement ring—he was still married—and brought Izabela to the county registrar, where they paid for a marriage license. For an immigrant, this cemented her citizenship, but the license was never picked up (nor was it valid). At her last appearance at the bookshop she frequented, Izabela was spotted with Robinson, purchasing a number of books and announcing that she was now married to him. Izabela also informed her parents that she was married, but it is unclear whether this was another orchestration by Robinson. By the summer of that same year, Izabela had disappeared. To cover his tracks, he told one of his hired web designers that she was caught smoking cannabis and was subsequently deported.

Dovetailing with Izabela's disappearance, Robinson convinced yet another victim into his BDSM desires. Suzette Trouten, a licensed practical nurse that moonlighted as a submissive slave. Again, using the Internet and the powers of his persuasion, he managed to convince Trouton to move from Michigan to Kansas so that the pair could travel and pursue their relationship.

"Suzette Trouten had told her family that she was going to work for a wealth businessman who did a lot of international traveling," Detective Wilson said. "And that she was going to take care of this businessman's ailing father while he traveled."

Like Clampitt's mother, Trouten's mother Caroline takes the bull by the horn and calls her "employer" when she has not heard from Suzette.

She is told that Suzette had run off with a man named "Jim" who was going to be sailing around the world with her.

"Suzette Troutten was a momma's girl," Lt. Rick Roth said. "Was always in contact with her mom either through e-mail or the telephone. Caroline knew that her daughter would call her and fill her in on what was going on. She knew something terrible had happened to her."

Again, Robinson mailed letters to cover his tracks, these letters purportedly to be from overseas, but postmarked with Kansas City postmarks. To further cover his behavior and Trouton's lack of correspondence, Robinson confided in her mother that she stole money from him and ran off with an acquaintance.

The Arrest of John Edward Robinson

"At the time he was supposedly running a business," Roth said. "That was basically a magazine for mobile home trailer parks."

The FBI and police were dumbfounded at how to build their case. They had missing women all connected to a two bit con man but had no physical evidence.

"We had to find all of these individuals," FBI Agent Dirk Tarpley said. "Make sure number one that they were alive and find out what find out what kind of contact he was having with them. What was he trying to do."

Suzette's mother would continue to receive letters. She knew that Suzette was not writing the letters as there were no spelling errors and the fact it "just didn't sound like Suzette."

Police were convinced, however, that Robinson was involved in her disappearance. They didn't want to start interrogating just yet. Instead, they began to question Suzette's friends.

"Suzette Trout was kind of a free spirit," Roth said. "She was into the BDSM lifestyle. She was always on the Internet with people in that lifestyle and she was ready to be on her own."

"None of us really knew anything about it (BDSM)," Roth continued. "So as we're conducting this case we're trying to learn about this lifestyle. Pain is part of this lifestyle. So slapping or spanking someone, that's natural."

Friends would reveal that Suzette liked to be the "sexual submissive".

She spend a lot of time surfing the Internet looking for a "master."

"She had come to this area at the behest of this guy named John Robinson," Lt Paul Morrison said.

John Robinson, however, did not look the part. He was a con man, yes. But a killer?

"Our impression of John Robinson was that he was a small-time con artist who was involved in a number of con schemes over the years," Daniels said. "But nothing really more than that."

But Robinson had a "side business", continually calling hospital and charity homes inquiring about helping out single mothers or other women in trouble.

Determined to not let Robinson off the hook, the FBI mounted an exhaustive investigation.

"We called in all the old retired detectives," Roth said. "Everyone who worked his cases before, trying to find a probation officer, we were looking into his (Robinson) background to find any clues that we could use against him.

The FBI began to focus on Tiffany Stasi, the baby. By the time they amped up the investigation in 2000, the baby would be fifteen years old.

And the FBI believed that somehow the baby would still be alive.

Initially, they believed that Robinson might be in some kind of baby-selling ring. An informant would come forward, however, and reveal that he would bird-dog women for Robinson. They discovered that Robinson would hire women for "photo sessions" and believed that he may have been selling this women into prostitution across international lines.

"It was hard to figure out what he was doing," Daniels said. "He was a con man on one hand but on the other hand he seemed to be involved in these other things which were darker."

The FBI was at a loss as they only had circumstantial evidence. They then put Robinson on twenty-four hour surveillance.

"We didn't want to tip our hand at any time to let Robinson know," Roth said. "If we contacted him, the gig was up and he would start denying everything and possibly sending us on goose chases."

They needed watch Robinson and wait for him to make a mistake.

They quickly learn he's living a double life. During the day, he is a family man with four kids. At night, he is with the underworld characters of topless bars and the like.

"We followed him to homes," Roth said. "We followed him to motels where he had women meet him there. The man was just in total action until five o'clock when his wife got off work."

"Robinson thought he was smarter and brighter than anyone else," Wright said. "That if he got caught he would just tell another lie as he had done for so many years and he didn't believe that there was anyone that was going to hold him accountable."

The FBI did a wire tap on his phone and subpoenaed records for his Internet usage. The FBI was able to log in to two Canadian women who were having real time correspondence with Robinson.

He was inviting the women over for BDSM sessions.

"To me he just seemed like a very commonplace little man who you would never suspect being involved in S&M type activities," Wright said.

"He referred to himself in the e-mails on the BDSM club website as 'master'," Roth said. "And that's what we knew him as. The 'Slave Master.'"

His modus operandi remained the same over the last fifteen years. He would seduce women with his BDSM techniques than promise them a job.

"He promised them the moon," Roth said. "And a lot of these women just took it, were hooked and came to Kansas City."

The FBI soon set up a stakeout at the motel where Robinson would indulge with the women he would import from out of town.

"They could hear talking," Wright said as the FBI agents listened outside his room. "A man's voice. A woman's voice. They heard what they thought were some slaps. We knew that he was into this BDSM lifestyle and that probably was taking place in that room. It was a really tense time for law enforcement because you knew somebody was getting hurt but the question was what was consensual and when did it cross the line."

Robinson's carelessness continued, perhaps as he felt more and more convinced of his abilities to evade authorities. Fortunately, he was not aware that he was building a case against himself while police carefully orchestrated a plot to track him down. His name was becoming linked to more than one missing person report. By 1999, both Kansas and Missouri began to implicate him as being involved.

His addiction to sex would prove to be his undoing as two women filed sexual battery complaints against him in June of 2000.

A woman named Brenda would come forward.

"She had come to town to work for a man she knew as James Turner," Roth recalled. "She was down on her luck, she was unemployed at the time, had no money."

When Brenda meets up with "James Turner", however, she realizes that she has gotten in over her head.

"One of the times they had gotten into an argument," Roth said. "She was struck by him. A little too hard. She had went up to the desk to inquire who had rented the room and she was told 'James Robinson.' So she knew that something wasn't right."

Brenda would go to police and accuse Robinson of sexual battery.

Another woman would come forward, filing an identical complaint against Robinson as well as robbery (he allegedly stole nearly $900 worth of sex toys.)

Buoyed by the two complaints, police now have enough to arrest Robinson.

Police arrested him at his rural property near La Cygne, Kansas.

"We were all a nervous wreck," Detective Wright recalled. "It was all very tense and a nervous time for everybody. He answered the door. We knocked on it. Was polite. You know, kind of carefree, invited us in. We told him that he was under arrest. We told him that we'd be investigating him for quite a while."

Robinson is arrested for sexual battery and robbery. But the investigators decide to question him about the missing women.

"Robinson turned pale," Wright recalled. "He started almost hyperventilating. I remember he turned back and looked at me (and said) 'Jesus Christ' like that and just kinda collapsed in the chair. I think it was a real shock to him and I think he knew would had him but when we walked him out of the house he picked himself back up and he was kind of back up and he was back to his arrogant self and he said 'you guys are making a big production out of this, aren't you?'"

The authorities confiscate his computers and get search warrants for the various storage units he has in four different cities.

"The Olatha storage locker proved to be a treasure trove of evidence," Lt Morrison said. "We found birth certificates, driver's licenses, social security cards belonging to several of these women. The kinds of things that you don't give up unless you're dead. It sort of confirmed what we were thinking all along and that is where are these letters coming from?"

They still had no bodies, however.

Searching his farm, a task force came upon two decaying bodies, hidden in eighty-five-pound hazardous-material drums.

"We actually were going to move the barrels out in order for the dog to get scent there," Roth said. "And when I rolled the barrel out and brought it upright, we saw blood coming out."

The bodies inside were identified as two of the missing women associated with Robinson: Izabela Lewicka and Suzette Trouton.

"We ended up finding Suzette's body," Wright said. "She was decomposed by then. You know, you're kind of sad because obviously she's gone but you're elated because you finally got something on this guy."

Following a similar lead across state lines, a Missouri task force searched a storage facility where Robinson rented two garages. It was there that police found three similar drums containing the corpses of Beverly Bonner, Sheila Faith and her daughter. All of the five women were murdered in the same way, with one or two blows to the head from a hammer. This was substantial and overwhelming evidence that Robinson was responsible for the death of these women—and perhaps many more...

Conviction

Just as trying to pin down John Edward Robinson proved a slippery affair, his conviction—or the one he deserved—proved somewhat elusive. In 2002, the state of Kansas sentenced him to death for the murders of Trouten and Lewicka, with life imprisonment for killing Stasi because her murder occurred before Kansas reinstated the death penalty.

Simultaneously, Robinson faced a complex legal dilemma in Missouri. Based on evidence discovered in that state, prosecutors were actively pursuing additional murder charges, yet Robinson's attorneys opposed his extradition because Missouri was more likely to push for capital punishment than Kansas.

Ultimately what the Missouri prosecutor Christ Koster wanted was for Robinson to lead investigators to the missing bodies of Lisa Stasi, Paula Godfrey, and Catherine Clampitt. Robinson refused on the strategy that any of this would lead to his further guilt in Kansas. Koster also faced pressure to offer the plea bargain, as it was unclear which state—or jurisdiction—the murders had occurred.

Robinson remained elusive to the end, and thus the prosecutors were put in the position to reach a compromise because the remains would likely never be found without his cooperation. In 2003, Robinson's carefully composed plea only acknowledged that Koster possessed enough evidence to convict him of five of the women: Godfrey, Clampitt, Bonner, and the Faiths. His statement was a guilty plea, but Robinson remained firm on accepting responsibility and was devoid of

remorse. Despite overwhelming evidence and public outcry, Robinson currently remains on death row in Kansas.

Aftermath

As it may be imagined, a life like the serial killer John Edward Robinson's leaves a swath of destruction that reverberates for all of the lives that he touched. Even for those who are only casually acquainted with the particulars of his case, it serves as a cautionary tale to the depravity of the human soul—or maybe the consequences for someone without one.

Surprisingly, throughout Robinson's whole ordeal and clandestine activities, his wife Nancy and their children remained unaware of his other life. Was his wife in denial, complicit, or simply unaware? For the mindset of Robinson, it's hard to form a solid conclusion on her involvement. In 2005, Nancy Robinson filed for divorce after 41 years of marriage, citing "incompatibility" and "irreconcilable differences."

Robinson's misdeeds with handing off Lisa Stasi's daughter to his brother and sister-in-law caused further pain and suffering. In 2006, Lisa Stasi's daughter (known as Heather Robinson since being illegally adopted) filed a civil suit against Truman Medical Center in Kansas City and against the social worker in charge, Karen Gaddis. Heather Robinson argued that Gaddis informed John Edward Robinson about Stasi and her newborn daughter in 1984; the claim rested on the idea that Gaddis didn't follow up on Robinson's legitimacy after he asked her he was looking for women for his fictitious home for "unwed mothers of white babies." It wasn't until 2007 that Heather Robinson and the hospital reached a settlement for an undisclosed sum, which Heather Robinson agreed to split with her biological grandmother, Patricia Sylvester.

***

While some serial killers tend to follow a sexual deviant's path, Robinson's con artistry added another level of questioning: was he truly a "master" of deviance, or were the mechanisms of the state to weed out individuals of his caliber insufficient? Worse, like his membership to the BDSM cult, were others equally complicit—and are they still among us?

In addition, for all the promise and freedom of the Internet, here was the antithesis, luring those who decided to pursue the more "free" realms of human interaction, only to be preyed upon by someone who had terrible designs for those that wanted to explore their sexual preferences. Nowadays, it seems commonplace to be mistrustful of those we meet online, especially with a whole proliferation of scam artists and predators.

Finally, for those among the sexual community of BDSM, a conviction of this sort casts doubt on the validity and consensual experience of those that choose to be a part of it. Can anyone truly trust one another after a killer like John Edward Robinson flew beneath the radar for so long? These are questions that color the very essence of experience as human beings seeking pleasure and reassurance. This is what a serial killer is truly capable of.

COLD BLOODED CHARMER : SERIAL KILLER SHAWN GRATE

34

JESSE DIXON

A desperate plea for help

On September 13, 2016, a call came through Ashland, Ohio's 911 system from a distressed woman, who claimed to be held captive in a home.

"I've been abducted," she whispered to the dispatcher. "Please hurry."

The police who arrived at the scene not only rescued the woman who had placed the call, but also discovered two dead bodies – left there by Shawn Michael Grate, a 40-year-old man who had a reputation for being a "cold-blooded charmer." Grate also brought police to a third body, located in a wooded area by a ravine in neighbouring Richland County. And, as the investigation continued, police uncovered connections to two more murders.

"(He is) obviously a serial killer," said Marion County Sheriff Tim Bailey. "It's hard to believe others aren't out there."

The cold-blooded charmer

"He was charming. He was always smiling, and he had those big blue eyes," said Amy Smith, remembering Grate as a teenager in Marion, Ohio. "All the girls liked Shawn."

As irresistible as he was, multiple women recall experiencing Grate's dark side early on. By the age of 18, Grate had revealed himself to be jealous, controlling, and violent – and was even arrested for grabbing the throat of his young girlfriend.

When he was only 23, Grate broke into the home his pregnant 17-year-old girlfriend, where he choked her and, according to Marion police reports, threatened to kill her. And only eight months later, he hid all night under the girl's couch before assaulting her and her sister with a butcher knife.

"(Grate) told them to shut up because he was in control," reported an officer at the scene. "Then he said if anyone comes to the door, there will not be anyone here to answer it, so you better hope that no one knocks at the door."

In addition to this pregnancy, Grate is known to have fathered at least two other children. Two were with girlfriends in Marion, and the third is the product of a brief marriage in Mansfield. According to court documents, Grate's ex-wife said he once threatened that "if I can't see my daughter, then no one will."

Grate's criminal history is fairly extensive – but until 2016, he'd only spent about four years in prison for a burglary in Marion, violating early release conditions with an assault, and for domestic violence. Grate had also been charged several times with offences relating to drugs and alcohol.

Grate grew up in Marion County, the product of a broken home. His mother, Teresa McFarland, left his father, Terry Grate, in 1982 – and eventually relinquished custody of both Grate and his older brother, Ronald, to her ex-husband.

McFarland still resides in rural Ashland County, and has discussed her son in only one interview to date. She told the Daily Mail, a British tabloid, that her son changed after getting involved with drugs and spending time in prison – and added that for the past three years, Grate had been estranged from the rest of the family.

"Yes, he's good looking, but the devil's good looking, too," McFarland said. "He ain't got no red horns and all that stuff. You find out he's charming, and of course, that charm can charm the pants off anybody."

It's this charm that Grate uses to get what he wants. He's been described as lazy by many people who have recently come in contact with him – and rather than work, people say he prefers to take advantage of kind, vulnerable people, particularly women with money.

Wally Toward, a businessman in Mansfield who owns several properties, saw Grate attempt to move in with several of his female tenants.

"Grate always mistook kindness for weakness," Toward said. "He exploited kind people."

By his late 20s, Grate was beginning to show signs of mental health issues. According to Smith, Grate's teenage friend, he would frequently invest all his energy into a project before completely giving up on it after only a couple of weeks.

"He would just give up on everything," she said.

His erratic behaviour was a concern to a female friend of Smith's, who had dated Grate around 1999 but eventually broke up with him because he "wasn't acting right."

"He would get very, very depressed," Smith said. "My girlfriend would say, '(he) is not wanting to get off the couch. It's been days.'"

In 2005, Grate started dating another young woman named Christina Hildreth. The couple dated for about five years, and eventually lived together in Crawford County.

"He was very handsome and quite charming," she recalled. "He had a way of looking at you like you were the only person he saw."

However, after they moved into the same residence, Grate began to reveal his controlling, jealous tendencies – and it was hard for Hildreth to deal with.

"He started showing a side of himself that was cold and indifferent," she admitted. "He wanted me to himself."

It wasn't just his relationships with women that escalated, however. Tim Denis, who used to be a close friend of Grate's, said the friendship fell apart over a bad loan. When Denis refused to provide Grate with financial support, he received a string of angry text messages from his friend – and admitted the last message "still gives him chills.

"Meet the other me," Grate had messaged.

A growing threat

Following the divorce of his parents, Grate lived with his mother in Marion County, where he completed high school in 1995. At that time, he was a close friend of Smith's, who said she remembers him as her "go-to person" and a "shoulder to cry on."

"He was the one that came to a Halloween party dressed as a woman, making everyone laugh and has nothing but a smile on his face," she recalled. "That is the Shawn I know. That is the Shawn I want to remember."

Grate was the literal boy next door for Julia Pennington-Smith, who graduated from River Valley in 1995. She remembers Grate as one of her childhood best friends – not as a serial killer.

"I knew him from the time I was five years old," she said. "We grew up together. We were neighbours. We went to school together. We used to play backyard football, we used to play softball. They were like my brothers; I loved the family."

While Pennington-Smith said she hadn't been in contact with Grate since they graduated from high school, the two were friends on Facebook.

"I don't remember him being troubled," she said. "I don't remember him ever getting into any trouble. He lived a normal life."

But Grate's first adult arrest happened just weeks after he turned 18, while he was still in high school. While his juvenile record is unknown, there are police reports available detailing his early run-ins with the law.

The first arrest was the result of a domestic incident, after his girlfriend at the time claimed she had been trying to end the relationship for the past six months. However, the couple was still together and had a new baby when she reported a second domestic incident in January 1996.

"He seems to be involved in nonviolent crime except when dealing with females, especially those he is intimate with," said Tristin Kilgallon, who teaches a class on serial killers at Ohio Northern University, where he works as an assistant professor of criminal justice.

Later that same year, Grate was convicted of a felony charge after committing a burglary with a juvenile, and was sentenced to four years in prison. He served only seven months and was released early – but his violence continued to escalate.

In 1999, when he was 22, Grate's 17-year-old girlfriend told police that he had choked her nearly unconscious – while she was two months pregnant with his child.

"(His girlfriends) are getting younger... why? Are they easier to manipulate?" Kilgallon inquired. "He chokes her – this is up close and personal."

Still, the incident resulted in less than a month's worth of jailtime for Grate. Although the teenage girl's family pursued a restraining order against Grate, the young woman had the no-contact order removed just a few months later.

Even after Grate's second child was born, the relationship continued to struggle. His son was born in September, and only a month later, Grate threatened his son's mother and her sister with the butcher knife. During the struggle over the knife, both Grate and the young girl sustained minor to severe cuts.

"He steps it up," said Kilgallon. "He's using a weapon now."

This incident meant a longer period of incarceration for Grate, as his early release was revoked in 2000 and he was forced to serve what was left of his original four-year sentence. The prosecutor on the case said a separate prison term was initially sought for the new conviction, but the judge sentenced Grate to probation only.

In January 2003, Grate was released from prison again – and by October, he was already in more trouble with the law. Another domestic charge came as a result of a complaint received from the mother of Grate's second child, stating that he had choked her and forced her to perform a sex act on him. No sexual assault charges were laid, but Grate was charged with two counts of misdemeanor domestic violence – and went back to prison until May 2004.

Grate mostly laid low for the next couple years, with records showing nothing but minor run-ins with the law – but Grate has admitted now that his first kill was in 2005, an unidentified woman who was distributing newspapers and magazines in his neighbourhood.

In 2005, Grate started dating Hildreth, who he moved in with a year later. He was upset that her children were living with them as well, Hildreth said, but said he was primarily just mentally abusive – although she does recall some physical violence, as well.

The worst incident happened in June 2010, Hildreth said, when Grate assaulted her repeatedly – with multiple blows to her face, and grabbing her roughly by the throat. She even fractured her hand in an attempt to defend herself from the falling blows.

Grate did eventually bring Hildreth to the emergency room, and they told the hospital staff that she'd fallen. However, as soon as she was left alone with a nurse, Hildreth explained what had actually happened. While police were informed immediately, Grate managed to escape arrest temporarily – but was arrested four days later, when Hildreth told the authorities that she was concerned Grate was hiding inside her couch.

Grate was charged with a first-degree misdemeanor domestic violence, and received a sentence of 180 days in jail. Despite the issuing of a protection order, Grate continued to call Hildreth from jail, and sent letters that he addressed to her cats. Hildreth, however, ended their relationship after incident, and to this day, believes it kept both her and her children alive.

"Before that night, I feared he would kill me," she recalled. "That night only strengthened that fear. I now believe more than ever had I not left him, I would be dead or one of my children would be."

The family man

Grate settled down with a new partner in 2011, a 28-year-old Mansfield woman named Amber Nicole Bowman. The couple were married and living together in the ranch house she owned when she gave birth to their daughter in July 2012.

Despite her young marriage and a brand new baby, though, Bowman filed for divorce in October 2012, citing "serious and unfortunate differences" in the separation agreement filed in December of that year.

Bowman sought a restraining order just a few months later, in April 2013 – claiming Grate had been calling her at work and making threats that if he couldn't see his daughter, "no one else will." He demanded money from Bowman, to "help him get back on his feet." He was also not paying child support for any of the three children he had fathered so far.

That June, the Richland County Child Support Enforcement Agency informed the county's domestic relations court that they had reason to believe that Grate was unemployed, and by September, a contempt of court order was issued against him for failure to seek work. He'd apparently been moving from place to place in Mansfield, but was technically homeless.

"He was not mentally disabled, he was not physically disabled," Toward said, who frequently worried Grate would steal rent money from his female tenants. "He could hold a job if he chose to, but instead of that he always chose to maneuver people to con them into helping him."

During this time frame, Grate was getting to know two women – Rebekah Leicy and Candice Cunningham. Leicy was a prostitute who worked in the Third Street area, the same area where Grate's ex-girlfriend Amber White used to work.

"He picked me up, I used to prostitute," White recalled, adding that he would only have about $10 or $20 to spend on sexual favours. "He was shy. He didn't talk (during sex), and he wanted the lights off. I was mean to him because I was strung out on drugs and he just disappeared."

Originally, Leicy's death was ruled as a drug overdose when her body was discovered in March 2015, in a wooded area of Ashland

County. After speaking with Grate following his arrest in September 2016, however, police have reopened the case and are investigating the possibility that Grate may be responsible for her death.

Cunningham and Grate were living together in Mansfield when she went missing in June 2015. When he was arrested, Grate informed police that they could find the body of a woman near a burned out house in nearby Madison Township. The body has yet to be identified, but evidence indicates it is likely Cunningham.

Foiled

Grate claims he wanted to marry the woman who called 911 on September 13 – a call that led to her rescue, and his arrest. The abduction victim, who has yet to be identified, occasionally played badminton with Grate at her apartment complex in Ashland – until she was kidnapped and forced to endured two days of involuntary sexual activity before she was able to place a call to police.

The chilling 19-minute call reveals a terrified woman whispering to a dispatcher in a quavering voice – identifying Grate by name, describing a nearby laundromat, informing police that Grate was armed with a taser, and reassuring the dispatcher that she was not bleeding, "anymore."

"I'm in the bedroom with him," she said, her voice hushed. "I'm scared."

The abducted woman lived in the same area as one of the other women whose body police discovered at the home, 29-year-old Elizabeth Griffith. According to Griffith's friends, she and Grate had dated, and Griffith had been missing since August 16.

"The short time I talked to her she cried several times, just about life and how she couldn't find anyone to love her," Grate said in a rare interview from jail in October 2016. "She had a mental illness."

Police discovered her body stuffed in an upstairs closet in the vacant home, and another body in the basement – Stacey Stanley, a

43-year-old woman from Greenwich who had been reported missing only days earlier.

According to Stanley's son, Kurtis, she hadn't come home after going out for a coffee and stopping at a gas station with a flat tire. Grate said he "helped" the woman before taking her back to the home where he had been squatting.

"It is a sad situation, especially the way she died," said Stanley's uncle, Argil Stanley. "She was beaten to death. The cops said she was unrecognizable from the beating."

After police uncovered the two bodies inside the house, Grate admitted to killing another woman in Richland County, and proceeded to bring police to her body – the body believed to be Candice Cunningham. He confessed that he'd also killed Leicy and another woman whose name he couldn't remember, back in 2005. His first kill, he said.

While the abduction victim who called 911 has not been identified publicly, her family has spoken out about the incident – and claim they will never forgive Grate for what he put her through. The victim's father said the family was fully supportive of the death penalty, which Grate has admitted that he deserves.

According to the victim's brother, Grate preyed on the woman's faith to develop a relationship with her – and eventually kidnap her.

"If somebody wanted to be a predator, like this guy obviously was, he could just feed off that and sense that," said the victim's brother. "As long as she would have somebody who would listen to that, oh, he could do whatever he wanted, manipulate however he wanted. That's the way I pretty much believe it went down."

Grate did admit to police that he is religious, as were a number of his victims. He said the women were lonely, and seemed to have lost their way – even claiming that they didn't even want to go on living.

In a confession, Grate explained that he would hug his victims and remind them that "we are all in this together," before choking them.

According to Grate, he would give his victims one last opportunity to beg for their lives – and if they didn't, he would end it for them.

So far, Grate has admitted to killing five women, and claims four of them were "choked out." His first victim, however, was stabbed in the throat. Grate believes her name was Dana, but her body has not been identified yet.

According to Grate, "Dana" delivered magazines and newspapers throughout his mother's neighbourhood in Marion, Ohio – but was "scheming" his mother out of her subscription.

"I remember her trying to sell them to me," Grate recalled. "Me and my mom would be on the porch and she'd try to sell them. My mom said she wasn't getting her subscriptions delivered."

Since he had company coming over soon, he didn't have time to strangle his first victim. Instead, he stabbed her in the throat and left her in the basement. Eventually, he brought her body out to Victory Road in Marion, where it stayed until it was discovered two years later. Currently, the only information the Marion County sheriff's department has to help make an identification is a sketch.

Grate also confessed to killing Leicy ten years later, although her death had already been ruled as drug related. According to Grate, the two had met at a bar, and she'd tried to steal $4 from him while he was in the restroom – so he strangled her, like the other three more recent victims.

Cunningham was killed in a vacant house the couple was squatting in, according to Grate, and he went back and burned the house down to hide her body. Police records show that the house had been destroyed in a suspicious fire on June 21 – the day after Grate successfully fled an officer who'd stopped him on a felony child support warrant.

"We were seeing each other for about seven months," Grate said of Cunningham. "She was pretty violent and suicidal, I turned her into a psych ward for about a week. Then we fought at the house in Richland for three to four days. Then the next day we'd get up and go for walks.

She could have run off and told police at any time ... She would take handfuls of pills at a time and I would give her the water."

Police are still collecting evidence and DNA to connect Grate to all five murders. Currently, he's been indicted on 23 charges – including aggravated murder for the deaths of Stanley and Griffith and kidnapping for the abduction of the victim who escaped. Each murder count carries the possibility of a prison term of 15 years to life, and the kidnapping charge could be punishable by 3 to 11 years in prison.

Charges have not been filed on the other three murders Grate claims to be responsible for. According to Ashland County Prosecutor Chris Tunnell, a "large volume" of evidence has been collected by the state Bureau of Criminal Identification and Investigation, the Ashland Police Department, and other agencies.

"A clear vision of WHY."

About a month after his arrest, Grate sent two letters to a Cleveland reporter, acknowledging his part in the five killings – and providing what he claimed was his motive for murdering the women. The letters were a response to a request for an on-camera interview.

"That sounds scary in facing myself even more," Grate's first letter stated. "The mirror has been enough but having more questions hitting me straight on could and would only help to understand me better."

The second letter explains Grate's motive for committing a "horrible act of violent behavior," stating that while in jail, he was able to gain a "clear vision of WHY."

"They were already dead, just their bodies were flopping wherever it can flop but their minds were already dead!" Grate wrote. "The state took their minds. Once they started receiving their monthly cheques."

Grate blames "government assistance" for robbing his victims of their "minds," and said that while he applied for government assistance five years ago, all he received was a $197 food card over a year and a half.

"Many bodies received 700," he wrote – using the words "people," "victims," and "bodies" interchangeably throughout the letters.

The letters are also full of Bible verses, specifically passages from the Book of Revelation and Hebrews.

"I feel I deserve the death penalty," he said in an October 2016 interview from prison, "but I also feel I can help some people in here ... I'm just trying to free myself of what I've done. I'm afraid of the death penalty ... I'd like to die on my own and not by the state."

Grate's mother, McFarland, said that she feels terrible for the trauma her son inflicted on his victims – and their families.

"it feels like a nightmare," she said. "I pray for the families. It's like a death to me too, and I have to grieve."

Jekyll and Hyde

Grate has claimed he feels some remorse for the murders – "50/50," he told a reporter.

According to Kilgallon, Grate is a perfect example of a killer motivated by a need for power and control. Often, he said, these killers are intelligent and charismatic – and master manipulators. When manipulation tactics fail, however, they will turn to violence.

Kilgallon added Grate was successful in covering his tracks each time, and despite frequently physically and sexually abusing his partners, they stayed with him – sometimes even for years. While Grate may have a specific victim type, he may prey on specific women simply because he finds them "easy targets."

"What we know about men, specifically that are violent against women, is that they feel entitled to be violent or justified in their violence," said Nancy Radcliffe, HelpLine of Delaware and Morrow Counties' director of sexual assault services.

Radcliffe's experience in the area of intimate partner violence spans more than 25 years, and while she has not assessed Grate's case personally, said he may fit the "Jekyll and Hyde" model of domestic abusers.

"On the outside, on any given day, they seem to be very outstanding members of society – people that you would look up to or wouldn't be at all threatened by," she explained. "But there's this other persona that comes out from time to time, and usually towards the person that they want to see it."

Toward, who claimed he's always prided himself on his ability to read people, admitted that he "missed the boat" when it came to Grate. And while he has had confrontations with a number of people during his time delivering subpoenas for local attorneys, he doesn't like to think about the fact that he made have had some "vivid discussions" with a potential serial killer.

"When I look back and try to analyze why I could not read him was because he is truly evil," Toward said. "For every Mother Theresa, there's a Charlie Manson – and he is Mansfield's Charlie Manson. He is a sociopath. You can't read a sociopath because there's no soul to read."

SERIAL KILLER PETER SUTCLIFFE

BRUCE CANDELO

48

<u>The Yorkshire Ripper</u>

The Yorkshire Ripper was- is- perhaps the most famous British serial killer, aside from his Victorian namesake. His crimes gripped the nation over a five year period, starting in 1975. But behind the media image created for him was a man called Peter Sutcliffe, a normal man from the accounts of all who knew him. He first worked as a gravedigger, before moving on to regular jobs as a salesman, a factory worker, and finally an HGV driver. Nothing out of the ordinary.

Sutcliffe's story is one of inept policing, media frenzy and unrelenting brutality- and insanity. When initially apprehended, Sutcliffe claimed that he had been ordered to murder prostitutes by no less an authority than God himself. Because of his string of crimes, Sutcliffe has been imprisoned for almost the entirety of his adult life. He has no chance of ever being released.

What made him famous?

The murders took place over the course of five years, and grabbed the public's attention, in particular the murders of women who were not prostitutes. His victims were invariably women, mostly young women; almost all were stripped to some degree, and almost all had been murdered with some combination of a hammer, a knife and a screwdriver. Everything pointed to the work of a serial killer.

Besides the *modus operandi*, the bodies of the victims also pointed to a depraved murderer. Many had been toyed with after their death, slashed with knives or glass. One had been raped. As can be imagined, the murders captured the public's attention because of their depravity and violence. National newspapers complained of how long it was taking police forces to catch the killer.

In fairness to the police, however, they had been led down the wrong trail by faked evidence. Incredibly, the case was put back- maybe even by several years- by the fact that a member of the public decided to send letters and voice messages to both the media and the police force investigating the Ripper. The perpetrator of the hoax has since been named 'Wearside Jack', because of his distinctive Wearside accent.

In the tapes, he said: "I'm Jack. I see you are still having no luck catching me. I have the greatest respect for you, George, but Lord! You are no nearer catching me now than four years ago when I started. I reckon your boys are letting you down, George. They can't be much good, can they?" Based on the accent of the man in the tape, the police assumed that the man they were hunting was from the Sunderland area; Sutcliffe sounded nothing like him.

What took so long?

The case was being investigated by West Yorkshire Police, the regional authority. They were widely criticised by the media and the government for their inadequate treatment of Sutcliffe's case. Even though the search for the Ripper was the biggest undertaken by any police force in the UK until that point, they had failed catch the killer, largely because of their own reluctance to act on suspicions and the leads they had found. And most remarkably, he had been under their noses all along.

Sutcliffe was interviewed time and time again by police in their search for the Ripper. He had been flagged up as suspicious, but nothing had been done, largely because his accent did not match the one that could be heard in the Wearside Jack tapes. Despite that discrepancy, one junior police officer named Andy Laptew had been particularly convinced that Sutcliffe was his man.

"I wasn't happy with Peter Sutcliffe, there were a lot of alarm bells ringing," he told an interviewer in a BBC documentary. "The reason we actually went to see Sutcliffe was because his vehicle had been sighted in three separate red light areas. He had a striking resemblance to the photo-fit of the woman who was attacked in Buslingthorpe Lane, in Leeds. He had a gap in his teeth which again was indicative of the attacker of two of the women who were killed," Laptew said.

Even his job was in the suspect occupation group, since Sutcliffe was an HGV driver at the time. Despite how well Sutcliffe matched the suspect, however, the police force was (for some reason) reluctant to act on their suspicions. "I said to my colleague, 'why don't we bring him in?" and he said 'no, we have been told specifically: do not bring anybody in," Laptew said in his interview.

He went on, "In fact, I'll tell you what happened. I took it direct to Dick Holland." Holland was the Superintendent in charge of the enquiry. But Holland was also reluctant to act on Laptew's hunch, despite how well Sutcliffe matched all descriptions and even the photo-fit. His reasoning was that Sutcliffe was from Bradford, a city with a completely different accent to the one they had heard in the fake voice messages. "Then (Holland) said, 'If anybody mentions the photo-fits to me again, they will be doing traffic for the rest of their service.' I could have crawled under the crack in the door."

In total, the police force interviewed a grand total of more than 40,000 people in their search for the Ripper. The vast majority of these were interviewed in the Wearside area, based on the voice of Wearside Jack. The real Ripper lived in Bradford, over 70 miles away. The fact that so much police time was wasted, and several lives lost because of one false lead, puts the Wearside Jack tapes at the top of the list of most damaging hoaxes in the search for any killer.

The beginnings of an obsession

While the police carried on with their manhunt in entirely the wrong part of the country, the Ripper carried on murdering women. For a description of his crimes, Sutcliffe himself is a remarkable source. He has spoken to the press and made highly descriptive confessions which leave no doubt about either his guilt or his capability of doing evil things. He begins his confession to police by explaining how his obsession with killing prostitutes began, and how eventually his hatred transformed into the desire 'to find a prostitute to make it one more less' as often as he could.

He went into gruesome detail, about each and every one of the crimes he had committed. He first described his assault of Wilma McCann, a prostitute local to Leeds. He said that actually, at first, he didn't realise she was a prostitute; all he knew was that she was thumbing a lift. But when she asked him if he 'wanted business', he 'decided to go with her'.

He then describes her impatience with him- he 'was expecting it to be a bit romantic', but she had changed her tone and asked 'what are we waiting for? Let's get on with it!' Sutcliffe described how he was put off, and Wilma stormed off to find another customer. But then, suddenly, he was overcome with rage- he ran after her, wanting to hit her.

He asked her not to go, to which she shouted back at him: 'Oh, you can f***ing manage it now, can you?!' This only made Sutcliffe angrier, and she carried on up the hill. In a fit of rage, he went back to his car, where he had stored his toolbox in the trunk. He found his hammer, and took it with him.

After eventually convincing her that he was ready, Peter got her to stop- but rather than doing what Wilma expected, Peter hit her brutally with the hammer. She crumpled to the ground, and he ran back to his car in a panic. He sat in the car for a while, wondering what he should do, when he noticed her arm moving.

He realised that to get away with what he'd already done, he would have to finish the job. So, he went back to his toolbox in the trunk, to pick out a carving knife. Why he had a carving knife in his toolbox is unclear, especially since he claimed that he committed the murder on the spur of the moment. That being said, the wounds inflicted on the victim matched what Sutcliffe described.

The Ripper's Spree

It was this murder which spurred Sutcliffe's hatred of prostitutes, in order to justify to himself what he had done to Wilma. According to the man himself, his next murder was not long after the first; this time around, he searched specifically for a prostitute that he felt would be an easy victim. He went back to the same city, Leeds, and picked up another woman, killing her with the same hammer that he had used to kill Wilma.

Sutcliffe said that he wasn't sure, but that he still may have had the same hammer in his toolbox by the time he was finally caught. It could have been another hammer that he says he bought specifically for the purpose of killing. Besides his hammer and his knife, he frenziedly attacked this second woman with a screwdriver to make sure she was dead.

All of the other attacks meld into one long, horrible narrative. His third victim he killed with a hammer and a box cutter, which he recalls he later lent to somebody. At this point, Sutcliffe said, 'killing prostitutes became an obsession' that he couldn't stop, 'like some sort of a drug.' His next victim was the one that grabbed national headlines and made the public pay attention, since she was only sixteen years of age, and wasn't even a prostitute.

In October, Sutcliffe murdered Jean Jordan, this time in Manchester. He murdered her in the exact same way as his previous victims, and left her for dead under a row of bushes. A few days later, he realised, the case had not been featured in the news; so incredibly, he decided that he could go back to the scene of the crime to retrieve the £5 note he had given her. But on not being able to find the note, Sutcliffe was "cursing the girl and [his] luck", and decided to take it out on Jordan's body.

He tried cutting off her head with a blunt hacksaw, but gave up quickly; he then took a pane of broken glass and slashed at her exposed stomach, which ruptured. Sutcliffe said in his confession that it "made [him] reel back and immediately vomit... it was horrendous." Realising that he was achieving nothing, he kicked her a few times and drove away.

His next victim, Yvonne Pearson, he hadn't even had to search for: she, not knowing who he was, had come to him. Again, he hit her with his hammer. This time however, a car pulled up next to his as he was dragging her away, and he had to hide with Yvonne- who was still alive- behind an abandoned sofa. This was the murder that suggested even to Peter that he was descending into madness, since after stuffing her throat and mouth full with straw and grass, to keep her quiet, he apologised to her... Even though she had already died.

These were just the first few victims of a number which eventually reached thirteen in total. This, also, is not counting the number of girls that he attacked but who survived. Other victims, he raped before he killed, and soon after his murder of Yvonne Pearson Sutcliffe started feeling an urge to kill any women, not just prostitutes. This, he described, was likely to lead him to be caught, but that in his subconscious mind this was what he really wanted.

Each of the murders that followed was increasingly reckless. The last two were murdered in broad daylight on suburban streets, as the victims walked home. Sutcliffe leapt from his car and beat them, in the middle of the sidewalk, before dragging them to a nearby yard to mutilate their bodies. In each of the last murders, members of the public seemed to get closer and closer to catching Sutcliffe in the act- but fortunately for him, they never did.

Arrest

Unbelievably, Sutcliffe was never apprehended during any of his crimes or in the process of disposing of one of his victims. He managed to completely avoid detection throughout his spree, and was only captured by chance.

Sutcliffe had had many prior scrapes with the police. Way back in 1969, he had assaulted a prostitute he had met during a search for another prostitute who had supposedly tricked him out of money. He got a lift from his friend to St Paul's Road, where he knew her to be; leaving the car, he walked out of sight. A few minutes later, he ran back to his friend, and asked him to make a quick getaway. In a later statement, Sutcliffe said that he told his friend: "I got out of the car, went across the road and hit her. The force of the impact tore the toe off the sock and whatever was in it came out. I went back to the car and got in it."

The prostitute informed police of the incident, and that she had seen the registration of Sutcliffe's friend's car. He was tracked down the next day, and interviewed. He admitted to having hit the woman, but denied using anything but his hand to hit her with. Fortunately for Sutcliffe, the woman didn't want to press charges since she was a known prostitute, and her husband was jailed for assault at the time.

This was just the beginning of Sutcliffe's terrifying spree. While this first victim was lucky, the 13 others were not as lucky; this first crime represented Sutcliffe growing in confidence, and hatred, and it hadn't been long until he learned how to kill. Unfortunately, it had taken police over five years to learn how to stop him.

During the police's search for the Ripper, they had interviewed Sutcliffe an incredible nine times. He was only finally apprehended when he was pulled over by police for driving with fake number plates in January 1981, long after his last murder. He was stopped by police, who had initially noticed that he was driving with a known prostitute, but the police check on his plates led the police to take him in for questioning.

The police noticed that he matched many of the descriptions of the Ripper provided by victims and witnesses, and so decided to question him in relation to the crimes. Police obtained warrants to search his house, and question his wife, and all evidence pointed towards Sutcliffe's guilt. After two days of highly intensive questioning, Sutcliffe confessed to committing the crimes. Based on what he said, the police found a knife, a length of rope and his famous hammer which he had discarded when pulled over by police.

He showed no emotion at all, apart from during the description of one murder, of a girl who was only 16 years old. He was accused of the murder of many women, although he denied the murder of one particular woman, Joan Harrison; it was later found that he had not murdered her, after all. After his confessions, which caused an intense stir in the media, he admitted that he felt he had been driven to murder by the voice of God.

Prison time

The case against Sutcliffe was open and shut. Because of his confessions, neither the courts nor the public were in any doubt that he had perpetrated the crimes of the last five years. However, he did try to convince the judge and jury that he deserved a reduced sentence, owing to a diagnosis of paranoid schizophrenia that he had received. However, he was unsuccessful, and was jailed for 20 consecutive life sentences.

Sutcliffe was jailed over 35 years ago, and has turned 70 years old since his arrest and imprisonment. He was first sent to a prison on the Isle of Wight, an island off the south coast of England. But only three years after being imprisoned, he was transferred to a psychiatric facility called Broadmoor. Broadmoor is famous in the U.K. as a high-security psychiatric hospital, which houses only around 200 people at any one time. While there, people like Sutcliffe receive psychiatric mediation and psychotherapy.

Sutcliffe remained at Broadmoor throughout his sentence, until August 2016 when he was transferred to Frankland Prison in Durham. The public feared that this suggested that he would eventually be released altogether, although Secretary of State for Justice Jack Straw told the House of Commons that there were "no circumstances in which this man will be released".

Sutcliffe's time spent imprisoned has not been happy. He was attacked by a fellow prisoner at Broadmoor, Paul Wilson, in 1996; Wilson had gone into Sutcliffe's room on the pretence of borrowing a videotape before attempting to strangle him, before two other inmates- including another serial killer, Kenneth Erskine- intervened.

Just a year later, Sutcliffe suffered another attack. This time, the attacker had more success. Ian Kay had intended to attack Peter with a razor embedded in a toothbrush. "I was going to ... walk into the room and cut his jugular vein on both sides and wait there until he was dead," Kay admitted to court.

"Killing has always been in my mind, ever since I've been here [at Broadmoor]. In hindsight, I should have straddled him and strangled him with my bare hands... He said God told him to kill thirteen women, and I say the devil told me to kill him because of that." But rather than attack him with the razor, Kay stabbed him repeatedly with a pen. Sutcliffe was blinded in his left eye, and his vision in his right eye was severely damaged.

In 2003, Sutcliffe fell ill and it was discovered that he had developed diabetes during his time at Broadmoor. In 2007, he was attacked again by Patrick Sureda who attempted to blind him in his other eye. Sutcliffe was sat in the dining hall, eating his lunch, when Patrick lunged at him with a regular cutlery knife. He missed, as Sutcliffe lunged backwards, and the blade stabbed him in the cheek instead.

What about Wearside Jack?

While Sutcliffe was in prison, the hoaxer behind the Wearside Jack tapes was also apprehended. In 2005, a review of cold-case files led the police to a man named John Humble was found to have sent the tapes. The tapes were sent in 1978, which makes the police's work all the more impressive- and made Humble 59 years old by the time he was finally tracked down.

By the time of his later life, Humble was a rapidly aging alcoholic. According to police reports, it took several hours for him to sober up enough after his arrest to actually submit to questioning. In explanation for what he had done, Humble claimed that he was inspired in equal parts by a desire for notoriety and a burning hatred of the police force, in relation to an incident earlier in his life where he was arrested for assaulting a police officer. Humble was jailed for nine years for perverting the course of justice, but was released after just four.

He had been a labourer his entire life, and had attempted suicide numerous times due to both guilt and what he felt had been a failed life. He told a national newspaper after his release that it had all been a prank, but it had gone too far, and that he hadn't realised the extent to which his hoax had affected the investigation.

Sonia Sutcliffe

Alongside the story of Peter Sutcliffe is the story of his wife, Sonia. Incredibly, Sonia stayed married to Peter for over a decade after his imprisonment. It was only in 1997 that she remarried a local hairdresser that she had met. Supposedly, Sonia had never known that her husband was a murderer despite his five year spree; the only two people who know the truth are Sonia and Peter themselves.

Sonia has won several high-profile cases against newspapers who she claimed had libelled her. She famously won £600,000 (around $1million adjusted with inflation) from the satirical magazine Private Eye, prompting the editor to claim: "If this is justice, I'm a banana." On appeal, she was only awarded a tenth of the initial settlement. Using the money, she moved into a new flat with her new husband in 1997, still living in the same area of Yorkshire as she had all those years ago. In many other cases of British serial killers, the house that they used to occupy is often bought by the council and demolished, or otherwise razed to the ground. This is to prevent shrines or museums popping up to exploit the sick fame of the murderer who used to live there.

It would have seemed that the perfect opportunity to do just that had come up when they moved out, but neither Sonia nor Peter wanted to sell their old home. In fact, Sonia Sutcliffe and her new husband moved back to the house that she lived in with Peter all those years ago in 2005. Through all the years since she had moved out, she had refused to sell the house- although if Peter did agree, the money wouldn't go to him, but to the Legal Aid Trust, a body that helps fund attorneys for those who can't afford them.

The motive may have been financial, since the property is worth at least half a million dollars and property prices in the UK increase consistently year on year, and Peter would probably never agree to losing half of that value. Their reasoning one way or the other is up for debate, but either way, it's difficult to imagine how Sonia can comfortably live there.

As British newspaper the Daily Express put it- "To this day she parks her car in the garage where Sutcliffe stored the 30 weapons, including hammers, spanners and screwdrivers, he used to murder 13 women in a six-year killing spree. She cooks her meals in the kitchen that houses the sink in which he once washed the bloodied clothes he wore while carrying out his depraved crimes."

Moreover, Sonia still visits Peter in prison, despite her having remarried. Peter has complained to the press that she doesn't visit him as often as she used to, and blames Sonia's new husband for the development- Peter claims that he's jealous and possessive. Even so, she still visits him month by month.

Yet more killings?

The worst thing about Sutcliffe is that even since being put in prison, the number of women he is suspected of having murdered keeps rising. Since being put in jail, Sutcliffe has been interviewed in connection with another 17 unsolved cases which are strikingly similar to the attacks he has admitted to.

Many of the list of unsolved cases involve hammer attacks, which were one of Sutcliffe's trademarks. One of the attacks was on Tracy Browne, who was attached in 1975 at the age of just 14. She was hit repeatedly with a hammer in the small town of Silsden, in West Yorkshire- in other words, in the exact same area as Sutcliffe's other attacks. She is still alive today, perhaps because of good fortune: she claims that her attacker was scared off by a passing car's headlights.

Another attack, from a year prior, is also thought to have been the handiwork of Sutcliffe. Gloria Wood was older than many of the other victims, at 28 years old; she too was hit with a claw hammer, by a man who she later described to police as bearing similarities to the Ripper. The man had offered to help her with her shopping bags before brutally attacking her. A third victim linked to Sutcliffe was Maureen (or Mo) Lea, who was also hit with a hammer- she was also beaten and stabbed with a sharpened screwdriver, just like other victim of Sutcliffe. That attack took place in late 1980, just a year before Sutcliffe's arrest.

Sutcliffe has not been charged with any more murders since he was put in prison. Considering that his sentence will see him die in jail, there seems little need other than closure for the victims of these crimes to investigate the cases.

SERIAL KILLER JOSHUA WADE

CRYSTAL DOWNS

Joshua Alan Wade is known for being a serial killer, hailing from the state of Alaska. At least five deaths are attributed to him, though it is widely speculated that there may be more victims. The following is a roughly chronological account of his life, with special emphasis on what is known about his upbringing, as well as his two most documented murders and their subsequent murder trials.

Joshua was born on March 18, 1980 to his mother Catherine and his father, Greg "Bubba" Wade. Bubba is an excommunicated Mormon who was once ordained as a church elder in the Melchizedek priesthood. Bubba and Catherine were, at the time, devout Mormons living in San Diego when their first child Mandy was born in 1978. Two years later, the family moved to Montana, where Bubba was hired as a Security Officer at an Air Force base. Josh was born shortly after the family arrived to Montana in 1980. The Wades soon returned to San Diego, where Bubba was employed as an officer for the Humane Society. He then relocated the family again, this time to Washington state, where he once again found work as a security officer. He was fired from that job, and became a bouncer at a nightclub.

By this time, Catherine and Greg were no longer involved with the church. Bubba began to deal drugs and have multiple affairs, as he was surrounded by women, drugs, and alcohol in his work environment. Catherine had also been unfaithful with a coworker at the local sawmill, and had subsequently become pregnant with his baby. "When my dad found out, right in front of my brother and me, he put a gun to her head and kicked her in the stomach," Josh's sister Mandy recalled. Catherine carried the baby to term, and then gave the child up for adoption. Mandy reported that it was traumatizing for both children when their sibling was given up for adoption.

Josh has stated that between the ages of five and seven (1985-1987), he was repeatedly raped by a group of neighborhood boys while his mother was at work. This was never reported to police, and Josh never got help. In an interview with a reporter after he had been sentenced to life behind bars, Josh stated "I didn't want to talk about it. I figured if I could just bury it, at seven or eight years old, you know, if I could just bury it, it would go away eventually."

Bubba and Catherine divorced in 1987 after 10 years of marriage, when Josh was seven years old. Bubba moved to Anchorage in 1991 and found work as a deckhand and cook on a commercial fishing boat, leaving his ex-wife and his two children behind in Seattle. Josh had severe behavioral issues that were already visible at the age of 11. At that time, Catherine was struggling with alcohol abuse and had essentially given up on raising her children. "She partied a lot, and she couldn't control either one of us," Mandy recalled. "She put us in a lot of really bad situations." Mandy recalls that she and Josh were taken to strip clubs prior to their teen years, and Mandy herself ran away on several occasions.

Josh attempted suicide at age 10 by attempting to drown himself in a bathtub. This incident was followed by three months of inpatient psychiatric hospitalization. When he got out of the hospital, he was never brought in for any follow up treatment, against recommendations.

Before their parents divorce, Josh and his sister Mandy witnessed acts of domestic violence at the hands of their father. In one instance, Josh and his sister were forced to watch Bubba stick a gun in their mother's mouth. Bubba later confirmed this fact in an interview, and said he had discovered that Catherine was having another affair. Josh and Mandy (aged six and eight) were sitting in the backseat of the family car when this occurred. Bubba forced Catherine to drive the family to her lover's residence, whereupon Bubba went inside and violently beat the victim in his bed. "Someone dared screw around with my wife, knowing who the hell I am?"

In 1993, Catherine sent her troubled and delinquent son to Anchorage to live with Bubba, where his problems continued to escalate through his teen years. Catherine indicated to Bubba that Josh was either going to come live with him, or she was going to put him in a home for troubled boys. After his departure, Catherine then largely disappeared from the majority of her son's life. She does contact him intermittently in prison, and Josh's sister Mandy has stated that Catherine still struggles with feelings of guilt regarding the outcome of Josh's crimes. She has since remarried, has other children, and remains in Seattle.

"I remember my mom begging a social worker to help her because she didn't know what to do with him," Mandy stated. She recalled having the usual types of sibling fights with Josh, some of which were physical, but also recalled that one time, he came after her with a knife. "Josh was always troubled. He wasn't right. He needed help. He's always had anger problems. I don't know. Like I said, we had a hard life. He just dealt with it totally differently." Mandy has no criminal background and is now a married professional and mother of three.

It didn't take long after Josh arrived in Alaska for Bubba to see that his behavioral issues were out of control. "I just wanted him to do something, not lie around all day and steal from people or smoke pot. So, I bought him his own tow truck, and instead of using it to make money, he cost me money by running into a city vehicle with it."

Bubba stated, "I wanted him to be with me, and I did the best I could. But you can't support someone on a bouncer's wages, working evenings and stuff like that." He also complained that Josh would sneak out at night. "So I went back to work selling drugs. Because I thought at least I'd be around, you know?"

Things continued to get worse for Josh. Bubba tolerated his use of drugs (and some argue that he passively encouraged it). His method of discipline was to withhold food from Josh. This left Josh to scavenge for meals in garbage and dumpsters on the street. At ages 12, 13, and 14, Josh was living on the street on multiple occasions. This was confirmed by Bubba, who stated that being on the streets was Josh's choice and that he was always welcome back home. Josh was also getting high. He had been smoking pot since the age of 12, and his father had given up trying to get him to stop. "You couldn't keep him from using it," Bubba recalled with a shrug.

Shortly after moving to Alaska at age 13, Josh was again admitted to a psychiatric unit for self-harming behaviors. He was "mutilating himself," according to his defense attorney. In all, there were two or three additional drug treatment hospitalizations and mental health hospitalizations. In each case, the caretakers recommended long-term care, and in each case, the recommendations were not followed. When he wasn't in treatment centers, he was often in detention centers.

At age 14, Josh was on the streets looking for food, after having food withheld again by his father. It was during this time and at this age that Josh claims to have happened upon and killed local 38-year-old John Michael Martin, who was an unemployed man with schizophrenia. Martin's body was found in May of 1994, and had died from a gunshot wound to the back of the head. He had left a Village Inn restaurant at 2:30 am and was killed shortly after departing. Martin was well known at the Village Inn, as he had frequented their establishment for the previous five years. He was often seen there all times of day having coffee with his friends. There was no indication that day that he was upset or that anyone was upset with him. Due to a lack of leads, flyers were posted around town with Martin's photo. Josh admitted to killing Martin 20 years later, but has never stated any sort of motive.

By age 16, Josh was stealing drugs from his father's drug stash. By this age, he was focusing his violent tendencies on others, rather than on himself. "I found out he had done some home invasions and had cut people with a machete. He threatened a friend of mine in front of me one time, and I grabbed him by his neck, shoved him against the wall, and I told him never to speak to someone like that again," Bubba stated in an interview. Josh was also obsessed with the film "Faces of Death," which depicted people dying in various ways, often gruesome. He was a very talented and able artist, and would frequently draw cartoons depicting the murder of Bubba. Josh wanted to be a tattoo artist, and worked hard to hone his artistic skills. In addition to these cartoons, Josh frequently created drawings of naked women, usually with very large breasts, and occasionally with demon horns.

Josh was fastidious and neat - his room was clean, his bed was made, his CDs were in alphabetical order. His bed was made military-style. His appearance was presented with the same high and clean standards. He spoke in a deep, gravelly voice and had an unpredictable and explosive temper. One former neighbor said of him, "He gave me the creeps."

Two months after his sixteenth birthday, Josh was caught by police behind the wheel of a stolen car, in possession of both cocaine and a loaded, stolen, 9 mm semiautomatic handgun. Bubba bailed him out and assured the judge that he would be able to control his son going forward. He also had an armed robbery charge during his teen years, which Josh attributed to "retaliation for selling me bad acid."

It was around this same time during Josh's teen years, that a woman reported to Anchorage police that someone appeared to be spying on her in her hotel room, after noticing a small camera dangling outside her window. The cord to that camera led to the room above, where Josh was staying with his father. Upon questioning, Josh waffled but eventually admitted that he did it, stating that he was "curious."

This same year, Josh faced allegations for allegedly molesting a six-year-old girl that he babysat for. The girl reported that he had fondled her while she pretended to sleep. After the second incident, she told her mother and said she didn't want Josh to come over anymore. Bubba had pressured the girl's mother into allowing Josh to babysit her daughter, stating that he needed a way to earn money. When the girl's mother confronted him, Bubba said he "intimidated her" into not pressing charges.

Bubba has stated that he doesn't see any remorse in his son; that the only remorse he sees is that he got caught. "Sometimes I wonder if it's something you inherit. Because I know that there's....a specific coldness about myself. The way I could react to people."

Josh was raised in a broken home, he was angry with his mother, his father was absent, he was sexually abused at a young age, he was using drugs before his teenage years, and was in trouble with the law shortly thereafter on multiple occasions. According to experts in the field, he fits the profile of a psychopath due to these factors. His sister and father state that he hates women, and both suspect that his actual number of victims is larger than five.

He appears to target Alaska natives. "Some of it may be racially motivated," Bubba said in an interview, as he speculated about additional murders that may have occurred. "For some reason, he thought Mexicans and blacks were the cream of the crop or something, and he thought Natives were scum."

At age 19, Wade claims to have killed 30-year-old Henry Ongtowasruk, who, like Martin, was also mentally ill. Henry was born in a small village in Northwest Alaska. Henry's body was discovered in December in the Alaska Budget Motel in Fairview, Alaska. His body was found by a maintenance worker at the motel. It was determined that he had died two days before his body was found. Henry had stayed at this motel for up to a week at a time several times during the few years prior. Henry had a case manager, and his housing was paid for by the state.Like Martin, Josh never revealed a motive for this murder.

In the year 2000, wade first saw Della Brown, whom he would later admit to killing. He was driving with a group of acquaintances (who would later testify against him in his 2003 murder trial) when they came upon her unconscious on the side of the road, having ingested both alcohol and cocaine. One of the individuals from the group dragged her body off the road and left it by a small shed. The group then left, but Josh went back later alone. He smashed her head in with a rock and left her body in the nearby abandoned, trash-filled shed. It was later determined that his first assault on her was not fatal, and he went back intermittently to assault her more, both physically and sexually, until she was dead, and then continued to assault her both physically and sexually after she was deceased. He left her body half naked and brought a series of acquaintances by to view her body. It was one of these acquaintances who eventually came forward, and Wade was arrested. The acquaintances who did see the body were criminals also, and accordingly, their credibility was easily called into question by the defense during the trial.

During the trial, the coroner stated that Brown's skull had been crushed to the point where it had the consistency of a "bag of ice." Brown's hair had either been sheared or pulled out; and burnt matches were scattered near her body. Brown's case caught extra attention because she was fifth in a string of six missing women over a 16-month period, five of whom were Alaska Natives. Most of the women were intoxicated at the time of their deaths, and of all them were seen outside and alone during early morning hours. Three had been stabbed, one strangled, one drowned, and the sixth was Della.

Della was a 33-year-old bingo hostess who was raised by her grandparents. On the night of her death, Wade claims to have also murdered an unidentified man who was also present in the shed as well (though according to him, he disposed of the body elsewhere). Per his report, he knocked the man out, put him in the trunk of his car, and killed him by "stomping on his head" when he regained consciousness in the trunk and started making noise. Wade claims he went to get drinks while the man was in the trunk. In a phone interview with Alaska news station KTVA, Wade stated, "I drove out to the Valley, found a spot, took the guy out, took his clothes off, and shot him in the head two times with a shotgun and pretty much took everything from the shoulders up," Wade contacted Alaskan TV station KTVA several times over the years to provide interviews and information.

Della Brown was abandoned by her mother as a child, and was a victim of abuse throughout her life. She was living in a trailer park at the time of her death with a violent man, and was also struggling with drug and alcohol issues. However, she had close and strong relationships with her mother, whom she reconnected with in adulthood, as well as other family members. Detectives would later conclude that the matches found at the scene were used after the victim's death by someone showing "disrespect" to the woman's body by throwing lit matches onto her face. Semen was found in her vagina and anus. There was a cut on her thigh, and another cut above her knee. Wade told his friends he tried killing her by cutting her throat. There were indeed, as presented during the trial, multiple cuts on her throat. They were not fatal wounds, leaving Della after they occurred until she succumbed to her injuries.

Wade told two of his friends at the time that Natives were worthless and that he was doing a favor for any Native he killed. On one occasion, Wade confessed the murder of Della to an acquaintance. "Why did you do that?" According to this acquaintance, Wade replied, "I don't know. I don't know what's wrong with me. I just don't like Natives."

During the 2003 trial, the defense essentially argued that Wade was a "big talker" who was just trying to impress his friends, and who would say anything to do so, but that he had not committed the murder. No evidence was found to charge him with any other murders at that time. After extensive efforts by the defense, the jury acquitted him of the charges of murder, sexual assault, and robbery of Brown. He was found guilty of only one of the 13 charges against him: tampering with evidence. This charge provided him with a sentence of 6.5 years. The trial was lengthy and was widely criticized for lack of physical evidence, poor work by the prosecution, and a highly skilled defense team.

As an attempt to gain a confession prior to the trial, Josh was recorded by police and set up by his friends. In the recordings that were made unbeknownst to him, Wade refers to killing two different women who had gone missing in the area by pointing to their photos in a newspaper clipping, but their identities are not clear on the transcript.

After the trial, <u>Anchorage Daily News reporter Julia O'Malley contacted members of the jury</u>; three of them spoke with her under conditions of anonymity. They said they acquitted Wade of murder because although they felt Wade wasn't innocent, there wasn't enough evidence to prove it beyond a reasonable doubt. They also claimed that the prosecution's arguments were confusing and that presentation was sloppy, while the defense's arguments seemed clear and raised many doubts.

In his closing statement, Josh stated "When I was a kid, horrible things happened to me. I had no counseling for that, and I don't think there's anything wrong with that, but they want to make it seems like it's bad because I needed help because something bad happened to me."

Josh had confessed his crime to no fewer than seven people, but there was no murder weapon. There was a carpet knife found in Josh's room that was regarded as inconclusive evidence - it contained blood that had been mostly wiped away, and the DNA evidence was not specific to Della or Josh. In addition, the prosecuting DA for the case stepped down a month into the trial for health reasons, to be replaced with two newer attorneys (neither of whom had prosecuted a homicide before).

Josh served a bit of time and was set free.

In April of 2005, a woman named Lisa Andrews filed a restraining order against Josh. Lisa was actually the mother of a teenage girl that Josh had originally been dating, but then she began dating him herself. The two had a tumultuous ,off-and-on again relationship. Josh has stated that Lisa is the only woman he's ever loved. The order stated that Josh held Lisa against a door and punched the door with his other hand, leaving two holes in the door. She made her way to the bathroom and locked it, after which he punched the door and left a hole there as well. He took her cell phone from her forcibly and broke it, per the report. 11 days later, Lisa asked him to leave his house because she was concerned about her safety and his habit of stealing from her. He called her a string of expletives and said he would burn her house to the ground. Lisa is an Alaskan Native. Later, Josh would attempt to marry Lisa from jail so he could exercise spousal privilege, given that Lisa knew much about his criminal history. However, the marriage was legally barred and never took place.

In 2007, Josh killed his next-door neighbor in Anchorage, Mindy Schloss, not long after completing probation for the Della Brown case. One evening, he was particularly upset about his financial problems and work difficulties. He had had several combative exchanges with his supervisors, and had even gone so far as to walk off of the job. He broke into Schloss' apartment to rob her and found her there. He restrained her with zip ties, gagged her, and wrapped tape around her head. He procured her ATM card and PIN number, and placed her (alive, tied up, and wearing a bathrobe) into the backseat of her car. He then drove her more than an hour north, forced her into some nearby woods close to an abandoned cul-de-sac, and shot her in the back of the head. He burned her body afterward. Wade had told acquaintances in the days leading up to Schloss' death that he wanted to have sex with her.

He then returned to Mindy's home and made her bed. He stole her watch, and left her car near the airport. In the bedroom, Mindy's bed was made with military precision, with the corners of the sheets folded tightly in a meticulous fashion. Mindy's friend Gerri thought that was bizarre because Mindy slept restlessly, and she never made her bed.

In their search for leads, police were quickly directed to Mindy's neighbors house: They were loud, there were parties, and there were lots of young people coming and going at all hours.The police noticed two $500 ATM withdrawals using Mindy's card, from two different banks. These withdrawals occurred the day after Mindy disappeared. The cash withdrawals were in the early morning hours. During their investigation, using search warrants and DNA evidence, two pubic hairs that matched Wade's DNA were found on Mindy's living room carpet. They also found his DNA on the steering wheel of Mindy's car, and Wade's coat contained an ATM receipt that indicated his $500 withdrawal from Mindy's bank account. They found Mindy's watch in Josh's house, as well as zip ties that matched those that were left on her body.

The bedroom that belonged to Joshua Wade was spotless. The bed was carefully made, the carpet was freshly vacuumed, and even his porn collection was neatly lined up on a shelf. Two books were next to his bed: Harry Potter and the Half-Blood Prince, and Jeffery Deaver's "The Cold Moon," which is a novel about a serial killer. He had plug-in air fresheners, and his clothing was hung very carefully in the closet, with equidistant hangers. His clean, white sneakers were lined up perfectly in his closet. His artwork was also discovered. The detective on site noticed that the work was impressive but misogynistic, with more naked women with large breasts and the occasional demon horn posing seductively. Of note, in every case, the woman's eyes were left blank and white. Detectives also seized a binder of newspaper articles that Wade had kept from his first trial, detailing the murder of Della Brown and his ultimate acquittal.

Mindy had been a psychiatric nurse practitioner. Because he had used her ATM card to withdraw money from her account, the crime became a federal instead of a state issue, and Wade became eligible for the death penalty, as Alaska doesn't allow the death penalty at the state level. Unlike the Brown case, Wade was suspected immediately.

Two weeks after Mindy's disappearance, Wade asked his friend Christina Greaser for a ride home. Christina Greaser had been following news coverage regarding the nurse's disappearance, and was troubled. She was watching the news when she saw surveillance video of Josh using Mindy's ATM card, and she realized that he had left his backpack in her car, and that it matched the backpack in the surveillance video. She looked in the backpack, and found half a bottle of alcohol, a wallet that had his old prison ID card, headphones, a cassette player, a toothbrush, a bandana, a lot of bank receipts, and a cell phone that had pictures of a gun on it.

Christina called the police and told them everything she knew. Josh coincidentally showed up at her apartment within hours without realizing what she had done. He asked for a ride, and she made excuses and said no. He got angry and ended up leaving. Christina followed him on foot and was giving updates as to his location to a local SWAT team as they attempted to capture him.

Wade went to some nearby apartments, knocking on doors, and forced his way into one. A brother and sister occupied the apartment, and the sister was held hostage for a short amount of time. A negotiator tried to convince Wade to give himself up. At 11:40 am, he did. The hostage was released unharmed.

In interrogation, FBI special agent Thoreson attempted to get Wade to admit to using Mindy's ATM card. "We talked to Mindy," he said. "You what?" Josh said, and smirked and smiled. The investigator stated that he knew at this time that Josh was the killer. Mindy's body had been found in September, with a bullet and shell casing nearby that matched the model of Josh's gun.

"I wanted to so much to believe that he may not have committed the first one, and then here another woman goes missing that's had contact with my son" (regarding the murder of the nurse)" stated Bubba. "I was just devastated."

Instead of risking a trial that could potentially lead to the death penalty, Josh pled guilty to killing Schloss and also admitted to killing Brown. He did this in exchange for a life sentence without parole.

Josh had had a violent history behind bars as well. In August 2008, Wade was placed in the Special Housing Unit for choking another inmate and threatening to kill him. While incarcerated and awaiting trial, It's been reported that Josh kept a jailhouse diary detailing his crime against Schloss in violently and graphic detailed terms, including a story in first-person perspective about being abducted and tied up with zip ties. In 2009, Wade faced twin trials in state (murder) and federal (carjacking) court regarding the killing of Schloss. Wade was kept in special housing away from other inmates because of his "temper" and "rage" issues, including the attempted assaults of other inmates while in prison in Washington. In May 2009, one inmate filed a lawsuit and claimed that Wade sexually assaulted him when he lured him into his cell and forced him to perform a sexual act, under threat that he would "never see his family again." The lawsuit also claims this wasn't the first time Wade had assaulted this inmate, mentioning another incident dating to 2003 when both men were temporarily housed in Arizona as prisoners of Alaska DOC. The case was essentially thrown out; not because of lack of assault, but because of unimpressive documentation on behalf of the prosecution.

The trial proceeded into 2010 and concluded with his sentencing. During a testy exchange at his sentencing, Wade revealed that he had more victims but didn't give specifics; these were the male victims that were described earlier. In this exchange, U.S. District Court Judge Ralph Beistline called Wade heartless, selfish, and a coward, to which Wade angrily and emotionally replied, "Don't push it, man - what about the men?" Wade repeated the threat to the judge, and said "Don't act like you fucking know me, man", to which the judge replied that Wade's reaction was indicative of how dangerous he is.

Wade was sentenced to 99 years in prison for the murder of Schloss, and is not to be even considered for parole until he has served 66 years (at which time he would be 95 years old). At that time, he would be turned over to federal authorities to serve the remainder of another life sentence for committing a murder during a carjacking. "I deserve much worse," he said, through tears.

At his sentencing hearing, Wade read an 11-minute statement. "I'm kinda glad I got caught," he admitted. He also stated to both families, "I don't think you believe me, but I am sincerely sorry for what I did.

There's no excuse for it. I know I've made faces at you in court, and I apologize for that."

Wade referred to the abuse he suffered as a young boy before moving to Alaska. "My mother did the best she knew how to. I wasn't raped at age five through seven because my mom was sleeping around or smoking crack or drinking. My abuse took place while I was trusted in someone else's care while my mom worked a man's job to support her kids. A single mother doing right. I chose not to deal with those issues, with those abuse issues, but instead to bury them and allow them to fester and build into a murderous rage. Which ultimately resulted in a lot of pain and suffering for others. No. I chose to be what I am. I'm not a product of a fucked up childhood or upbringing. I'm the product of one who decided not to overcome the past and succumbed to a fate that I created for myself."

Later, in an interview with a reporter from jail, when she noted that he seemed both remorseful and angry at the judge, he said "I am a murderer. I do have a temper." "Which is the real you?," the reporter asked. "They are both a part of me. That's me. That is all me." He said in that same interview that he does not discriminate and he would never hurt a child. "Certain situations have come up in my life that have resulted in these two women dying at my hands."

In 2014, Wade fully admitted to killing three men as described above, which he had previously hinted about in his sentencing hearing. He admitted to these killings in order to strike a deal with prosecutors that would allow him to move from the Alaska prison where he was residing to a prison in Indiana. He felt he was being treated unfairly where he was. Investigators are not confident about the validity of his claims regarding the additional killings. Nonetheless, Wade was transferred in February of 2014 from Alaska to a federal prison in Terre Haute, Indiana. At this time, it was undetermined whether or not Wade would stand trial for the deaths of Martin and Ongtowasruk.

Wade told Alaskan TV station KTVA that killing "didn't really bother me," and that he didn't view himself as a serial killer. Wade is the subject of a book called "Ice and Bone: Tracking An Alaskan Serial Killer" by Monte Francis. It should be noted that the majority of direct quotes in this article from Josh's father and sister were taken from interviews that they provided to that book's author in 2014, and the remainder were found in various internet archives and news stories.

It has not been determined at this time whether or not Wade really does have additional victims. According to Assistant U.S. Attorney Steven Skrocki, "(Wade) has a degree of wanting to be self-important, a high degree of needing attention, and a very high degree of insecurity. He's also quite manipulative." He noted that anger and spontaneity were big things for Wade, as opposed to being methodical or planned.

Classified as an escape risk and as one of the "most assaultive, predatory, riotous or seriously disruptive prisoners," Wade was kept in solitary confinement while in jail in Alaska, and permitted one hour per day to exit his eight-square-foot jail cell for exercise. The warden of the Seattle federal detention center, where Josh resided in 2008 and 2009, said "Inmate Wade continues to display a poor attitude and difficulty controlling his temper."

Most who know Wade suspect that he left many more victims in his wake than we know about. His sister Mandy said as a teenager, Josh told her he murdered a clerk at a convenience store, but she never learned anything further. The FBI is confident Wade has killed at least five people. Wade's method appears to be killing out of spontaneous anger, rather than cold and calculated planning. He did not stalk his victims; rather, they were just unfortunate enough to cross his path. Wade has been behind bars for close to a decade, in Alaska, Indiana, and now Texas.

"Anger, personal gain, control, power...those are all elements of Joshua Wade's motivations," said Craig Ackley, Supervisory Special Agent. "This monster, who could just take somebody out into the woods and shoot 'em in the back of the head...resembles nobody that I knew. Nobody," Bubba said in an interview after Josh's second trial.

Wade denied to Alaskan TV station KTVA that he is a serial killer. Upon asking what he would say to those who disagree, Wade's advice for people who believe he's a serial killer was short and to the point: "Quit reading books."

ROBERT HANSEN

RAY DUNCAN

Robert Hansen was dubbed the "Butcher Baker" by the media after he kidnapped, raped and killed at least seventeen women with possibly more victims that have yet to be identified. The murders took place in and around his hometown of Anchorage, Alaska as Hansen would hunt down his victims in the woods with a variety of weapons. It would take over twelve years before authorities would finally capture and convict Hansen in 1983. His case would remain out of the limelight until a movie called "Frozen Ground" would be released, detailing his exploits with John Cusack starring as Hansen.

EARLY YEARS

Hansen was born to Danish immigrants in Estherville, Iowa in 1939. Both of his parents were strict and Robert would be crippled by shyness for his entire life. He had a stutter and a bad case of acne which left pockmarks on both of his cheeks. His father, Christian, was a baker and Robert would eventually follow him into the same occupation. But his father was not a positive influence on him, routinely belittling his son. Robert had no escape, he was bullied both at home and at school.

At school, he was the proverbial social outcast. He would walk down the halls with his eyes downcast and very few people even noticed him. He only had a small handful of male friends who kept him at arm's length and virtually no female friends.

He had no success whatsoever with the opposite sex, being alternately ignored and ridiculed. This rejection would evolve into a seething hatred of all attractive women as his sexual fantasies about them turned into violent ones.

With no outlet, he took up hunting and found solace in the woods, shooting at animals.

At the age of eighteen, Robert would join the United States Army Reserve and would serve for one year before being discharged. The army service would give him a bit of self-confidence as Robert now attempted to talk to women and ask for dates. But women were taken aback by his awkward nature, his stutter and his thousand-mile stare behind black-rimmed glasses.

With his military experience, he would find employment at a police academy in Pocahontas, Iowa as an assistant drill instructor. Once there, he began badgering a secretary for a date until she filed a complaint against him. He would eventually meet his first wife in Pocahontas, marrying her in the summer of 1960.

The marriage would not last. Only a few months later, Robert would be arrested for burning down a school bus garage.

The bullying and torment Hansen experienced during his high school years would prove to be too much. He had to somehow, someway get back at his tormentors. So even three years after he graduated he decided to go back to his old school and burn down the garage that housed the school bus.

He would be sentenced to three years in jail during which his wife would file for divorce. He would serve a little over twenty months before being released.

The arson episode would prove to be another step on the ladder to Hansen's eventual homicidal psychosis. He was showing all of the earmarks of a serial killer; arson and cruelty to animals. He had felt powerless his whole life but would act out in fantasies where he would have power...whether it was by starting a fire or shooting a deer. Eventually, this need for power would lead him to a deep-seated desire to have power over the women who rejected him throughout his life.

ESCALATING BEHAVIOR

Robert would test the waters of criminal behavior starting with petty thefts. He would be arrested several times for theft, looking to be growing into a small time criminal until1963 when he married his second wife.

Four years into their marriage, the couple would have two children and move to Anchorage, Alaska.

Robert would start work in a local bakery. Under his father's tutelage, he was a capable baker and hiring him was a no-brainer. But his co-workers found him to be a social misfit. He would brag to them about the strangest things, like his kleptomania and ability to steal things without getting caught.

JUST ANOTHER FACE IN THE CROWD

Hansen went out of his way to give off the appearance of a respectable citizen.

His neighbors liked him and he would set several hunting records in the area, decorating his home with the heads of big game and fish. He would open his own bakery in a downtown mini-mall, becoming friends with the regular customers and even servicing the policemen who came in for their morning donut.

No one, not his wife, children or his neighbors knew of the monster that lurked inside him.

But he couldn't keep the monster hidden long. In fact, the respectable front was just camouflage.

In 1967, Hansen would assault a young receptionist at gunpoint. He would plead no contest to the assault charge but serve very little time. A few months later, he followed a pretty eighteen-year-old girl home and again tried to sexually assault her.

He would serve very little time in jail, being sent instead to a psychiatric facility where he described his bizarre and dark sexual fantasies. He would tell his psychiatrist that he suffered from memory lapses and remembered little of what took place during his assaults.

The courts were lenient on Hansen to a fault.

In 1971, Hansen would kidnap and rape a seventeen-year-old waitress outside a coffee shop.

He would let her go but not without a threat.

"I will hunt you down," he hissed in her ear. "Hunt you down and kill you. I'm a respectable man. I own a business. You're just a kid. No one will believe you."

The teenage girl, scared out of her wits, believed him.

With no punishment or capture in sight, Hansen would become even bolder as he plotted out his mouth violent fantasies.

FIRST BLOOD

In what would seem to be a recurring theme for Hansen's victims, there was very little media coverage or follow-up investigations.

In 1973, a seventeen-year-old schoolgirl named Megan Emerick walked out of a dorm laundry room in Seward, Alaska and disappeared without a trace.

She is presumed to have been another of Hansen's victims though he would later deny it.

Unfortunately, Megan's disappearance would garner little in the way of press or law enforcement investigation. There were a few fliers and short articles in the local newspaper but little else offered.

Megan was a quiet girl who grew up in the peaceful town of Delta Junction. She liked to go out on the Yukon River to hunt and fish. A typical teenager, she liked rock music and horses but she left home at an early age to go to the Seward Skill Center, a place in Alaska where she would learn a vocation.

But on July 7th, she would disappear.

Years later, the vanishing teenage girls would be part of a growing trend in the Eklutna and Knik River areas.

LOST IN THE FOG

As construction of an eight-hundred-mile oil pipeline began in Alaska, a different population began filing into Anchorage. The oil money brought in prostitutes, pimps, and drug dealers who sought to service the oil workers who now had money to burn. The community began a transient one and sudden disappearances became nothing out of the ordinary. Anchorage became a frontier town, a city full of strangers where people disappeared without a trace.

Robert would initially target any woman who caught his eye. But he began to learn that strippers and prostitutes were less likely to have people come looking for them. He would soon develop his own modus operandi, a system that he would adhere to with religious fervor.

He would target solitary women under the guise that he was a photographer, offering compensation if they posed for him. Hansen would then arrange a meeting place in a coffee shop and wait outside, making sure that the woman arrived alone. Once assured that there would be no witness, he would arrive at the coffee shop and convince the woman to come leave with him for the photo shoot. They would get into the car and he would already have one-half of the handcuff attached to the passenger side drive handle. Once he got into the driver side, he would lean over and in one motion handcuff their wrist and take out the gun from his glove compartment.

Sometimes he would drive the women home or to an isolated motel room where he would rape them. Other times he would fly to a desolate area along the Knik River.

A STRANGE CODE

Robert didn't kill all of his victims. Sometimes he would rape them and release the ones who he thought really found him attractive. His reasoning was, they played out to his fantasy and didn't deserve to die.

Others, the ones who resisted and fought, he would pretend to set free. Then he would hunt them down through the woods and shoot them with his rifle.

By the summer of 1980, bodies of dead prostitutes began to be found in and around the Anchorage area. But finding dead bodies in the Alaska wilderness was not an out of the ordinary type thing. Hikers would often get lost in the wilderness and not know how to make their way back, succumbing to the elements.

The first would be a young woman believed to be in her late teens or early twenties. Workers in a building found a shallow grave on Eklutna Lake Road. The body was badly decomposed and half-eaten by bears. Police were able to make a facial reconstruction from the skull and published their approximation of the young woman's appearance to the local news outlets. The victim was never identified, however, and to this day is still known as "Eklutna Annie."

When her body was recovered, she was estimated to be in her late teens or early twenties. She was between 4'11" and 5'3" inches tall with long, reddish-brown hair. Hansen would admit that she was the first victim that he killed but that he didn't know her name.

Hansen said that she or her family lived in Kodiak. Investigators believed that she may have come from Washington or California.

What is certain is that she was a topless dancer or a prostitute that Hansen picked up, offering to pay for her services. He told her that he lived in Muldoon but when Hansen drove past the town the woman panicked. She tried to escape out of his truck but Hansen pulled a gun on her.

"Now look," Hansen said. "If you do exactly what I tell you and don't give me any problem whatsoever, there's going to be none, you won't get hurt in any way, shape or form."

"Eklutna Annie" could only nod in agreement out of fear. They continued to drive, her heart racing with fear, her mind racing with strategies on how she could escape.

But then Hansen's truck got lodged in the wet Alaska mud. Hansen allowed the young woman to step out of the vehicle to help put the truck back on solid ground.

Then she ran.

Hansen stated that he caught her by the hair as she took a knife out from her purse.

Overpowering the young girl, Hansen wrenched the knife away and stabbed her in the back.

Her body would be found on July 21st, 1980 buried near a power line.

MORE BODIES...

Joanne Messina was another body found near Eklutna Lake Road, buried in a gravel pit. Her body was badly decomposed and there was little evidence remaining. She worked as a topless dancer as did other Hansen victims such as Sherry Morrow and Paula Goulding.

Sherry Morrow was a striking beauty, with feathered blonde hair and heart-shaped lips. She was an aspiring model who turned to topless dancing to make ends meet. Like he would do so many times, Hansen would meet her under the guise of a photo shoot.

Sherry would be among the first that Hansen would play the "hunting game" with. After raping and torturing her, he flew her to the woods where he sent her blindfolded and handcuffed, telling her to run.

His sadistic fantasies now coming to life, Hansen would hunt her down. He would follow her through the woods as she cried and begged for her life.

He shot her in the back, rolled her over and ripped off a necklace from her neck.

A 'good luck' arrowhead locket that her boyfriend had given her.

It was the next step in his mind, to begin taking mementos and trophies of his victims. He would set them aside in a box then when he felt the need to relive the moment he could take the souvenir out, fingering it through his hands and relive the fantasies in his mind.

UPPING THE ANTE...

The adrenaline high that Hansen got when he first began killing started to subside. So he began the 'hunting game' in order to feed the monster inside. He had gone from petty theft to attempted sexual assault before graduating to rape and murder.

Now it was turning the rape and murder into a sport.

Sherry's body would be found on the banks of the Knik River. Sherry had been reported missing for over a year and her body was found in a shallow grave on the banks of the river. Two off-duty police officers were in the wilderness hunting moose when they came upon her decomposed remains. She had been shot in the back three times with what investigators believed to have been a hunting rifle. Her body was fully clothed but there were no bullet holes in her clothing. Investigators believe that she had been naked when Hansen shot her after which he put her clothes back on.

Police were able to identify Sherry's body from dental records. She had been reported missing over a year ago by her boyfriend. The clothes they had found on her skeletal remains were the same as the clothes described by her boyfriend.

The case would go nowhere, however. The police told the boyfriend that the killer had over a year to cover his tracks. Finding him would be next to impossible.

Paula Goulding would meet the same fate as Sherry Morrow. Only seventeen-years-old and looking for work, the unemployed secretary started work as an exotic dancer to pay her rent. She would be targeted by Hansen and fall victim to him in the same way Sherry did. He would capture her, send her into the wilderness blindfolded where he would chase her down then after she couldn't run anymore, shoot her down like an animal.

Paula's body had been found in the exact same fashion, shot in the back but then redressed after death.

Sue Luna's body would be found two years later, the young Asian woman was forced to strip herself naked while Hansen made her run like a dog through the woods. The game was intoxicating to him as he shot her in the back after a lengthy chase.

Delynn Frey, Teresa Watson, Angela Feddern, Tamara Pederson, Lisa Futrell, and Andrea Altiery would all become victims of Hansen. He would collect "trophies" from each of them, taking a custom-made fish necklace from Andrea Altiery that would later be a critical piece of evidence when he would be captured.

But that capture when not come until June 13th, 1983 when Hansen encountered seventeen-year-old prostitute Cindy Paulson.

A STREET SMART STREETWALKER

Hansen was trolling for his next victim when he spotted Cindy selling her wares on an empty street. He had enticed Cindy to come into his car for $200 in exchange for oral sex. Cindy didn't feel threatened by the man, she got into his car without a second thought.

Hansen struck fast. He reached over and handcuffed her to the door then held a wood handled revolver to her head.

"Not a s-s-s-sound," the man stuttered as he put the car into drive. He drove her to his home in Muldoon. The alert Cindy began taking notes in her mind. The home was in a relatively well-to-do area. Once she entered, she found the home to be well kept and with nice furniture and full of hunting trophies. Hansen took her down to his den where there was a chain hanging from the ceiling. He tied her to the chain and stripped off her clothes. He would hold her captive for hours, alternating between raping and physically torturing her.

Hansen would grow tired and chained her by the neck to a post in the basement. Hansen then laid on the couch and went to sleep.

Upon awakening, Hansen untied Cindy and threw her in his car.

"If you t-t-t-try to get anyone's attention," Hansen hissed at his captive. "I will k-k-k-kill both you and them."

Hansen then bragged that he already had a rock solid alibi. He had convinced a friend to lie for him.

Hansen took his captive to the Merrill Field airport.

"We're flying out to my cabin," he snarled.

Cindy laid down on the back seat of the car, her hands cuffed in front of her body but her legs free. The car parked and she watched as Hansen began packing gear into his Piper Super Cub (a small two-seat airplane). Seeing her opportunity, Cindy scooted out of the back seat, opened the driver's side door and sprinted toward the nearest street.

Hansen turned around in time to see Cindy running but luckily for the young woman she made it to the busy street.

Robert Yount slammed on his brakes of his trucks on the rainy road. He opened up the passenger side door and picked up the young woman, immediately taken aback by her disheveled appearance. He drove her to the Mush Inn where Cindy ran inside, telling the clerk to call her boyfriend.

Yount would drive on to work where he called the police himself and told her about the half-naked, handcuffed woman he had dropped off at the Mush Inn.

Anchorage police officers arrived at the Inn but Cindy had disappeared. The clerk told them that she had taken a cab to the Big Timber Motel where her boyfriend stayed.

Police would go to the hotel and find her in room 110 of the motel. She was still handcuffed and alone. She told the police about Hansen, describing him as a wiry, scruffy man. He was tall at six feet but she thought he was non-threatening because he spoke with a stutter. She told of her hours of torture and rape, being hung up by her wrists and taken to the airport. The whole story sounded like something out of a horror movie but the detectives believed Cindy. She was street smart and scared out of her wits. The police drove her out to the hospital but then Cindy insisted on stopping by the airport.

Cindy was then able to positively identify the same plane that she saw Hansen toss weapons inside of. They also talked to a security guard who obtained the license plate of Hansen's vehicle. With a description and now an address in hand, detectives set out to Hansen's home.

Their suspect would arrive shortly after they staked out his home. Everything about him was exactly as Cindy described. He was wiry, nervous and spoke with a stutter.

As non-threatening as could be.

The inside of his home was also like Cindy as described. A moose head on the wall, trophies and news clippings of his hunting exploits.

A hidden panel in his wall would reveal a large cache of weapons.

All of this was legal, however. There was no evidence that Cindy had been raped. The only evidence was that she had been inside his home.

"I was at my friend's house," Hansen explained. "I was repairing a seat for my airplane then I went to the home of another friend. I left his house then went to the airport and installed the seat."

Hansen would deny Cindy's allegations during his interrogation. He deflected, stating that Cindy was telling them lies because he would not pay her extortion demands.

Hansen had an arrest record but his shy and quiet nature put some doubt in the mind of the cops. Police corroborated his alibi with his friend, John Henning, and the case went cold.

Cindy identified Hansen in a police lineup and insisted that he was the man who raped her. Things went south in the investigation, however, when Cindy refused to take a lie detector test. She had an inherent distrust of police and if they wouldn't take her at her word, she was willing to put the whole thing behind her.

She knew that Hansen was taking her on a one way trip to her death and she escaped. She also knew that the police didn't take prostitutes seriously.

So she walked.

She drifted in and out of the area and couldn't be reached when the police wanted to follow up. The case would be suspended.

But Detective Glenn Flothe of the Alaska State Troopers had already made the determination that the several bodies found around the area was the work of one man.

A serial killer.

And there was something about Robert Hansen that made alarm bells go off. He had a task force go out to the red light districts of Anchorage and warn the women that a serial killer was on the loose.

Then he got the FBI involved.

BRING IN THE BIG GUNS...

Flothe would team up with FBI special agent Roy Hazelwood in developing a psychological profile of the kind of man they were looking for.

Hazelwood believed that the killer was a man who was an experienced hunter but with low self-esteem. He would have a history of problems with women and would keep "souvenirs" of his kills such as a piece of jewelry or article of clothing. Hazelwood also believed that the killer would be socially awkward with a speech impediment.

Flothe used the profile and quickly narrowed down his investigation to Hansen. They would go to Hansen's home and bring him in for investigation. His team would then get a warrant to search Hansen's house, cars, and plane. They would discover jewelry belonging to the missing women as well as a cache of weapons hidden under the insulation in Hansen's attic. They would find the rifle they believed was used to kill two of the topless dancers as well as the revolver with the wooden handle he used to kidnap Cindy Paulson.

The mother lode, however, was an aviation map with little "x" marks all over it, indicating where Hansen had murdered his victims.

The search warrant was being executed at the same time that Hansen was placed into the interrogation room.

Investigators had decorated the room with pictures of his victims, maps of where they found the woman's bodies and crime scene photos.

They wanted to get inside his head, to let him know that they were on to him.

The man who psychologically tortured so many women was now having the script flipped on him.

INTERROGATION AND REVELATION

Another break in the case would come when the neighbor of Hansen noticed the police outside his home. She inquired as to what was going on and was told that Hansen was under investigation for murder. She quickly recanted her husband's story, stating that he had lied to cover up for Hansen and he did not know the extent of his crimes.

Investigators demanded an explanation of why Hansen had possession of the necklaces of the dead women. Hansen would deflect and deny until the interrogators finally cornered him. He would then get defensive, blaming the women and justifying his actions until he finally cracked.

"I started in 1971," Hansen said. "They were usually young. Like sixteen and nineteen. I didn't move to the prostitutes and strippers until later. I would get mad at them sometimes, sure. They would raise their prices on me."

Hansen would be arrested and charged with assault, kidnapping, multiple weapons possession as well as theft and insurance fraud (Hansen had filed a fake claim stating that someone had stolen his trophies. He used the proceeds to buy his private plane.)

Striking a plea bargain, Hansen would participate in telling the police about the markings on his aviation map in order to locate the bodies of his victims. He did this on the condition that they left his family alone and that it would not be publicized. An agreement was reached and Hansen would plead guilty to the murders of Morrow, Messina, Goulding and "Eklutna Annie".

"I began killing in the early 1970s," Hansen said. "Sometimes I would let the girl go. But only if she could convince me that she would not go to the cops."

Hansen would lead police to over seventeen grave sites. He would refuse to give up three marks on his map (two of these are suspected to belong to the spots where he killed Mary Thill and Megan Emrick, both of whom Hansen has denied killing.)

Hansen would be sentenced to 461 years plus life in prison without the possibility of parole. He would later be sent to the Anchorage Correctional Complex for health reasons and would die at the age of 75 on August 21st, 2014.

The identity of "Eklutna Annie" remains unknown.

STRANGLER JOHN

JOHN DENIS

93

John Reginald Christie was a prolific serial killer active in England during the 1940s and 1950s. He murdered at least six women including his wife—and some believe this number is higher, as well as a baby—before being arrested, convicted, and hanged. He lured women to his flat under the guise of assisting them with some medical procedure such as abortion and strangled and raped them; oftentimes while they were unconscious or dead, thus giving rise to allegations that he was a necrophiliac. Christie also likely framed his neighbor Timothy Evans for the death of Evans' wife and infant daughter for which Evans was convicted and hanged.

EARLY LIFE

John Reginald Halliday Christie was born in Halifax, Yorkshire, England on 8 April 1899. His father was a strict disciplinarian who was often abusive and mother and sisters were domineering. Yet, he was his mother's favorite so while Christie's father despised his frailty his mother emasculated him with over protection. His four older sisters also reinforced his mother's protective nature but they also dominated him. One incident when he was ten disturbed him profoundly; that of seeing one of his sister's legs up to the knee which made him physically attracted to her. This likely contributed to Christie's development into a controlling, sexually-dysfunctional hypochondriac with an intense hatred and fear of women because he simultaneously desired those who tempted him but, consequently, knew he could not satisfy them.

Christie's maternal grandfather died when he was eight and when asked if he wanted to see the body during the wake, Christie said yes. He felt pleasure and a release of the tension he always felt when the man was alive because his grandfather was rather frightening and these feelings fascinated him. He started playing in the graveyard and liked to look inside the cracks of the broken vault where children's coffins were kept.

In school, Christie did rather well and got along even though he did not cultivate any long-term meaningful friendships. At age 11 he won a scholarship to Halifax Secondary School where he proved rather adept at mathematics and algebra, and also with high-detailed work. He had an IQ of 128, was a scout, and sang in his church's choir; however, he grew increasingly unpopular with his classmates and was often ridiculed for his ineptitude with girls being given the names "Can't Make it Christie" and "Reggie no Dick." By puberty Christie had associated sex with dominance, violent aggression, and death which rendered him impotent unless he was in complete control. At this time he would also feign illness—becoming a hysterical hypochondriac—to get attention.

Christie left school at age 15 and became an assistant movie projectionist. When World War I began Christie enlisted as a signalman. He allegedly was rendered unconscious and temporarily blind by a mustard gas attack and lost his voice for three years; however, physicians attributed his blindness and muteness as a hysterical reaction instead of a true physical ailment. Thus, Christie's fear led to his hypochondria and he would exaggerate illnesses to avoid unpleasant situations. More simply, he was a coward.

After his stint in the army, Christie became a clerk. On 10 May 1920 Christie married 22-year-old Ethel Waddington from Sheffield. She was a plump, homely, passive, and sentimental woman who many believed was afraid of her husband even though he was mostly mute during this time. The couple looked down upon others and, subsequently, maintained a high degree of privacy but also seemed quiet and rather pleasant, devoted to each other, and to their dog and cat. His ongoing impotence with his wife led to his frequent visits to prostitutes—which began when he was 19—when she was out of town.

After they married Christie became a postman. He once stole some postal orders and was, consequently, sent to prison for three months. Following his first period of incarceration Christie regained his voice during a temper tantrum with his father only to lose it again for six more months before being able to speak again. When he was 25,

Christie was placed on probation with the post office after being charged with violence and accused of frequenting prostitutes. Christie subsequently left his wife and moved to London while she remained in Sheffield with her relatives.

Four years later, Christie was sentenced to prison for nine months on theft charges. Following this prison release he went through multiple jobs and lived with a prostitute who he physically assaulted with a cricket bat to the head and returned to prison for six more months. He was suspected of assaulting other women; however, the lack of evidence resulted in no arrests. A few years later he stole a car from a priest and was arrested again. After being released from prison this time he asked Ethel to move to London with him so they could be a married couple again.

Thus, in 1933 after a ten-year separation—and lonely at age 35—Ethel rejoined her husband, unaware of the type of man he really was or how her life would take a tragic turn.

Soon thereafter, Christie was hit by a car and required hospitalization which fueled his budding hypochondria. The literature suggests that over the course of 15 years Christie visited two physicians 173 times.

The Christies moved to the ground floor flat at three-story 10 Rillington Place in the Ladbroke Grove neighborhood of Notting Hill. At the time they moved here, Christie was a 40-year-old quiet inconspicuous man with reddish-ginger hair, light blue eyes, and an enormous forehead.

With World War II on the horizon, Christie signed up as a volunteer member of the War Reserve Police and became a Special Constable for Harrow Road Police Station for the next four years. Had his prior record been investigated—which it wasn't—there is no way that Christie would have received this appointment. Regardless, these four years were among Christie's happiest and he became almost fanatical about enforcing the law—so much so that he earned the nickname, "The Himmler of Rillington Place." Christie enjoyed wearing his uniform so much that the authority he had inflated his ego to the extent that he began to follow women and take notes of his endeavors. He also bored a peephole into his kitchen to watch his neighbors and ran down every single transgressor, no matter how minor the offense.

When his wife went to Sheffield to visit her relatives Christie developed a taste for peculiar sexual activities and found women who responded to his advances. One woman Christie met worked at the police station with him. She had a husband overseas in the war and Christie often spent time at her house with her. When her husband returned unexpectedly he filed for divorce and named Christie as a co-respondent after beating him up upon finding Christie in his house.

After this Christie began bringing women to his flat.

But first...

Timothy Evans

In the spring of 1948 Timothy and Beryl Evans moved into the third-floor flat. They were newlyweds and expecting their first baby. Timothy was 24 and Beryl was only 19; he drove a van for a living and was functionally illiterate. Known for his excessive drinking and often violent temper—likely due to his small stature of five-foot-five and 140 pounds—as well as his IQ of 70, propensity for lying, and proneness to self-aggrandizement, the Evans frequently quarreled. When the baby arrived—they named her Geraldine—Timothy's substandard income and Beryl's poor housekeeping and mothering skills caused them to fight even more, sometimes resulting in mutual physical violence. Beryl allegedly told Mrs. Christie that Tim had tried to strangle her and that she was pregnant again with an unwanted child. Beryl tried unsuccessfully to get rid of the baby.

It was around this time—the end of October 1948—that workers came to fix some floors and walls of 10 Rillington Place, as well as the community wash house.

In early November Beryl and Geraldine disappeared. There were conflicting accounts of their disappearance and subsequent murders; however, what is known is that that Christie offered to help Beryl with her pregnancy "problem" around noon one day. He is reported to have used rubber tubing to gas her for the procedure but she allegedly panicked so Christie began to hit her, and then strangle her, and then tried to have intercourse with her. When Evans came home that evening, Christie told him that the abortion hadn't worked and that if Evans went to the police it would only get them both in trouble and that police would not react well to reports that Evans and his wife fought often.

Christie proposed that he would dispose of Beryl's body and he hid her into the second-floor flat that belonged to Mr. Kitchener who was in the hospital at the time. Evans allegedly fed Geraldine and told Christie that he wanted to take his daughter to his mother's house but was dissuaded by Christie who told him that it would arouse too much suspicion. Christie told Evans that he knew a young couple who would take Geraldine and that Evans should tell people that Beryl and Geraldine were out of town on holiday.

Some speculate that Christie strangled the baby and put her with her mother in the second-floor flat and then blocked out what he had done.

Christie then told Evans to sell his furniture and leave town which Evans did.

Once the workmen were finished in the wash house Christie moved the bodies and hid them there. The following day he visited his doctor complaining of back pain. Despite Christie being a hypochondriac he had never had back problems. The doctor concluded that it was an injury sustained by unaccustomed exertion such as lifting a heavy weight.

Evans' mother Mrs. Probert did not buy her son's account that his wife and daughter were on holiday and discovered that her son staying with her sister, awaiting his wife. Mrs. Probert knew Evans was lying, that Beryl and Geraldine were missing, and that the furniture had been sold from their flat. After being confronted Evans stated that he disposed of his wife and put her body down the drain. He said that did not kill her and did not want to mention Christie because of the additional problems that would have caused. Evans said that he had met a man who gave him some medication to produce a spontaneous abortion but told Beryl not to use it. He said that when he returned from work he found her dead, took care of his daughter, and then pondered what to do next. Evans stated that he put his wife's body down the drain outside of the front door, stayed home from work, went in to give notice, and made arrangements for someone to take of Geraldine.

Police determined that Evans could not have disposed of Beryl the way he claimed to have done and he was arrested. During his interrogation and subsequent investigation Evans claimed that that he simply helped Christie put Beryl's body in the second-floor flat and that he had inquired of Christie about his daughter but was told that it was too soon to see her. Police searched the building and garden and in Evans' apartment near a pile of papers there were clippings from the newspaper about "a sensational torso murder, known as the Stanley Setty case" which was odd because Evans did not read, as well as a stolen briefcase.

During Evans' interrogation the Christies were also interviewed, she being coached by her husband.

Police went back to 10 Rillington Place and searched again. This time they found the decaying corpse of Beryl Evans, wrapped in a green tablecloth and tied with cord in the wash house, hidden behind some wood propped up against the sink. Underneath some wood behind the door was Geraldine's dead body with a man's tie still around her neck.

Dr. Donald Teare, the Home Office pathologist, performed the autopsy which showed that both had been dead about three weeks.

Beryl had bruises on her lip and right eye consistent with being hit and that she had been strangled with some type of a cord. There was no evidence that she had ingested anything to try to abort her three-month fetus but her vagina had bruising. The pathologist did not take a swab to check for semen.

Additional interrogations yielded different stories by Evans. He first admitted that he did, in fact, kill them both and that he was relieved to confess. He said he killed his wife because she was running up debts and then killed his daughter a few days later after he quit his job. On the days Evans said he hid the bodies, the carpenters were still working on the wash house so this could not be true. Further, his confession contained words that were beyond Evans' intellectual capacity and that if he had sold all of his furniture like he claimed then the baby's pram and highchair would not have been in Christie's flat—an indication that Evans expected to see his daughter again. The next confession was even longer and contradicted the first one. After Evans' mother came to see him following his arraignment he insisted that "Christie done it."

Evan's trial began on 11 January 1950 at the Old Bailey for the murder of his daughter although evidence of his wife's murder was included in the testimony. Prosecutor Christmas Humphreys wanted to avoid any testimony such that Beryl may have provoked Evans which could possibly warrant a reduced charge of manslaughter with a lesser sentence which is why he only pursued Geraldine's murder; because it was without motive and clearly cold-blooded. Christie was Humphreys' chief witness in the proceedings.

Evans' defense was in the hands of Malcolm Morris from Freeborough, Slack, and Company; however, there was little investigation done to assist Evans, likely to save on time and money. They also failed to question the carpenters and friend Joan Vincent, and neglected to look into Christie's criminal record; all of which may have provided the jury with reasonable doubt.

During the trial witnesses such as the carpenters and Mrs. Christie changed their testimony from their original statements to "fit" Evans' confessions with respect to dates and times. The furniture dealer wasn't contacted either which would have demonstrated that Evans was only following Christie's direction and that Christie had, in fact, lied. Compounding Evans' troubles was that Christie's composed persona on the stand impressed jurors due to he was articulate, reflective and presented himself as the victim. His demeanor was diametrically opposite Evans' "apparent dazed and guilt-ridden presentation." When Morris brought up Christie's criminal past the court was impressed with the fact that he had been on the straight-and-narrow for the past 17 years. Little did the court know what Christie had really been doing during that time.

It took the jury only 40 minutes to reach a guilty verdict Evans was sentenced to death and was hanged on 9 March 1950. He would later be granted a posthumous pardon after Christie's trial when the truth was revealed even though some still believe that Evans did murder his family.

The Crimes

Mrs. Christie wanted to move since the only other tenants in the flat were Jamaicans against whom she was highly prejudiced. Further, after Evans' trial Christie went into a deep depression and lost a lot of weight, and also lost his post office job due to courtroom testimony about his past crimes. Ever the hypochondriac, Christie checked himself into a psychiatric hospital for three weeks and continued to visit his doctor for stress-related symptoms; 33 times in eight months.

He found work as a clerk with the British Road Service and things seemed to improve; however, Christie soon gave notice, citing that he had found a better job which was not true. His wife was not pleased with him being unemployed and around the house all the time. On 11 December Mrs. Christie watched television with a friend, on the 12th she took laundry to Maxwell Laundries, and then was never seen again.

Nobody said she appeared to be distraught or that she said that she was going to take a trip.

Christie told her friends that she went to Sheffield and that he would follow shortly as he had a new job there. He told family members that his wife wasn't feeling well enough to write them.

At this same time Christie began to sprinkle his house and garden with disinfectant due to the increasingly putrid odor.

In January, Christie sold his furniture along with his wife's wedding band and watch. For more money he forged his wife's signature on a bank account she had and emptied it.

Shortly thereafter Christie met a Mrs. Reilly who was looking for a place to rent and he showed both her and her husband his flat. They paid him three months' rent in advance and kept his cat. Christie borrowed a suitcase, had his dog put down, and left. The Reillys ultimately left when the impending investigation commenced and they were told that Christie did not have the authority to sublet his flat.

Investigation

One of the upstairs tenants at 10 Rillington Place—Beresford Brown—noticed a hollow space behind a kitchen wall in Christie's old flat after the landlord gave him permission to use the kitchen since the flat was empty. Brown was looking for a place to mount a shelf for his radio and pulled away some of the wallpaper to try to open the door which he couldn't. When he shined a light through a crack he was horrified at what he found and called the police.

Chief Superintendent Peter Beveridge was on scene, as was Chief Inspector Percy Law of Scotland Yard, other officers, and the coroner. When the door was opened in the kitchen alcove they found a woman's corpse sitting in some rubble. Her back was to them and she was leaning forward. Behind her was something large wrapped in a blanket that was knotted to the victim's bra. Said bra was pulled up around her neck along with her black sweater and white jacket. Other than that she was nude save for a garter belt and stockings. She was taken from the cupboard and photographed and examined in the front room. She had been strangled with a ligature and her wrists were tied in front of her with a handkerchief tied into a reef knot.

Authorities focused on a second large object behind the woman and discovered it was another corpse. It had been propped on its head up against the wall. The blanket had been fastened with a sock tied in a reef knot around the ankles and the head was wrapped in a pillowcase that was also fastened by a stocking in a reef knot.

They noticed a third object. It was another body, also upside down, with her head beneath the second body. This one's ankles were tied with an electrical cord fashioned into a reef knot while a cloth covering her head was similarly knotted.

Investigators also took note of some loose floorboards in the rubble and found the wrapped body of Mrs. Christie amidst the rubble.

The first victim was a 20-something brunette who had been deceased for approximately one month. She had died from carbon monoxide poisoning and strangulation with a smooth type of cord. She had been sexually assaulted either at the time of her death or shortly thereafter. Scratches on her back indicated that she had been dragged across the floor. She was later identified as Hectorina McLennan, a 26-year-old prostitute.

The second victim was also a brunette and around 25 years of age. She, too, exhibited symptoms of carbon monoxide poisoning; particularly her pinkish skin color. She was also strangled and had had sexual intercourse around the time of her death. There was also evidence that she had been drinking heavily the day she died. She had poorly manicured hands and feet and was clad in a cotton cardigan and vest while another vest was fashioned into a diaper between her legs. It was estimated that she had died eight to 12 weeks earlier. She was later identified as 26-year-old Kathleen Maloney, also a prostitute.

The third victim was a mid-20s blonde, also poorly manicured, clad in a dress, petticoat, bra, cardigan, two vests, and another cloth fashioned into a diaper. She had also been poisoned with carbon monoxide and strangled. She, too, had been drinking before her death which was also eight to 12 weeks earlier and this victim was six months pregnant. She, again, a prostitute, was identified at Rita Nelson, 25.

The final victim—found under the floorboards—was a woman in her 50s, plump, and missing several teeth. She was rolled up in a flannel blanket with a pillowcase over her head. She was also wrapped in a flowered dress and silk nightgown and wore stockings. She had been dead approximately 12-15 weeks. She had been strangled by ligature but unlike the others there was no evidence of gas poisoning or sexual intercourse. She was identified as Ethel Christie.

Additional evidence found in the flat included potassium cyanide, a man's tie fashioned into a reef knot in the kitchen cupboard, a man's suit under floorboards of the common hallway, and a tobacco tin that contained four clumps of pubic hair; none of which belonged to any of the victims. From where Christie obtained the hair has never been resolved.

Police also found a human femur in the garden supporting a wooden trellis. Additional bones were uncovered in flowerbeds and beneath an orange blossom bush along with blackened skull bones with teeth, pieces of a dress, a newspaper fragment dated 19 July 1943, hair and teeth, and one skull. The coroner determined that there were two female corpses although only one skull had been found.

Forensic evidence enabled these last two victims to be identified as 21-year-old Ruth Margarete Fuerst who had arrived in England from Austria in 1939 and had disappeared 24 August 1943. She was around five feet seven inches with a tooth crown identified as being from Germany or Austria. When she disappeared she had been living in Notting Hill. The second victim was presumed to be Muriel Amelia Eady, 32, who had worked with Christie in a factory. The hair in Christie's garden matched hair from her former home. The black wool dress she was wearing when she disappeared matched remains in Christie's garden.

After Christie's failed affair with the woman whose husband was overseas, he didn't have any problems finding women who would, in fact, appreciate his attention. One day in a bar he met Fuerst. She worked in a factory and was also rumored to have been a prostitute. When Mrs. Christie was away she began to visit Christie at his home. One day in bed, Christie received a telegram telling him that his wife was on her way home with her brother. Christie alleged that Ruth had undressed voluntarily and asked him to have sex with her and then they could run away together. He stated that he refused and strangled her while they were having intercourse. He wrapped her in her coat and put her under the floorboards in the parlor until after his brother-in-law left and Mrs. Christie went to work. Christie then put Fuerst in the wash house and began to dig in the garden. That night he buried her in the garden. He found some of her clothing peeking up from the shallow grave and burned it.

It is hypothesized that Christie's lifelong hatred for women and repeated humiliations caused him to act the way he did. By strangling his victims he was able to exert some semblance of power and this was erotic for him as he was only able to achieve potency with women who were helpless: that being unconscious or dead. He admitted that after he killed Fuerst he experienced "a strange, peaceful thrill."

Christie met his second victim, Eady, in the company canteen as they both worked in the same factory. In October 1944 when his wife went to Sheffield to visit relatives Christie lured Eady into his house by telling her that he had a first-aid background from when he was with the War Reserve and could help her with the catarrh (mucous buildup in her nose and throat) from which she suffered. To avoid a struggle he was prepared with a contraption that resembled an inhaler with friar's balsam in a jar to mask the gas smell and a hose connected to the gas supply. Eady sat in a chair with a scarf over her head and as she inhaled, the carbon monoxide took effect; thus enabling Christie to strangle her with a stocking while simultaneously having intercourse as she was dying. He recounted experiencing the same peaceful thrill he had with Fuerst. Christie hid her body in the wash house and dug a shallow grave near the first. Later he found a broken femur bone while gardening and used it to prop up the trellis—something the police had not seen when they were investigating Timothy Evans for his wife's and daughter's murders.

Necrophilia is defined as having sexual relations with the unconscious or dead and keeping them close. There are three identified types. One is the violent variant wherein the perpetrator has an overwhelming urge to be near a corpse so they kill in order to satiate this urge. Often the individual visits the corpse where it is dumped and in some cases there is repeated sexual contact. Another type is the fantasy necrophiliac who makes death a central aspect of his or her erotic imagery. These types may ask a partner to play dead or take pictures of him or her looking dead so they can masturbate later. Christie is a textbook fantasy necrophiliac because, as mentioned, he was unable to perform absent the violence when he murdered his victims. He also had a violent necrophilia orientation in that he did, in fact, keep his victims nearby: in the alcove in his flat, under the floorboards, in his garden, and in the building's communal wash house.

Arrest

After Christie left his old flat he placed his borrowed suitcase in a locker and wandered around London. On 20 March 1953 he checked into a room at the King's Cross Rowton House with his real name and address. Despite booking seven nights he only stayed four. When a photograph of him emerged wearing his raincoat he purchased an overcoat from another man and gave him his raincoat instead. While he claimed at trial that he was in a daze, aimlessly wandering around London, his actions demonstrate that his contriving a disguise of sorts proved otherwise. He also claimed that despite news stories about corpses found at his house, he did not connect them with himself.

Out of money, Christie took to sleeping on benches and in movie theaters and was spotted by a police officer on 31 March near the Putney Embankment of the Thames River. After giving the officer a fake name and address, Christie was asked to remove his hat and was, subsequently, recognized and promptly arrested. On his being were his identification card, his Union card, an ambulance badge, a ration book, and an old newspaper clipping about the Timothy Evans trial with details about the murders.

Christie willingly gave his statement about four of his murders. He hinted that he couldn't remember something, essentially making the police "show their hand" by admitting that they did, in fact, find the two bodies in the garden. With respect to his wife Christie claimed that she had awakened him one night and she was choking; her face was blue. He tried to restore her breathing but she was suffering so badly that he got a stocking and strangled her to put her out of her misery. He then said that the bottle containing the phenobarbitone tablets he had been prescribed for insomnia was almost empty and he realized that his wife took the pills to kill herself. After leaving his dead wife in their bed for a couple of days he put her under the floorboards, admitting that he thought this was the best way to put her to rest and keep her close to him.

He managed to make the other three women's murders not his fault either. Since they were prostitutes he claimed that they were the aggressors, demanded money, and forced themselves into his flat. He claimed Nelson picked up a frying pan to hit him and they struggled and she fell into a chair "that happened to have a rope hanging from it." When Christie came to from his alleged blackout she was dead. He said he left her there overnight and in the morning—after he had a cup of tea—he wrapped her up, diapered her, and shoved her into the alcove cupboard.

With respect to Maloney, Christie said that he met her in a café and she went home with him and threatened violence and only remembers her being on the floor and that he put her into the cupboard. In reality, he gassed her, strangled her, had intercourse with her, and then diapered and wrapped her body.

Christie stated that McLennan and her boyfriend needed a place to stay so he invited them to live with him. He asked them to leave after "several uncomfortable days" and she had come back one night, struggled with Christie after he asked her leave; however, some of her clothing tore and got wrapped around her neck. He said he sat her in a chair but she appeared to be dead so he put her in the cupboard.

The numerous psychiatrists who evaluated Christie while he was in Brixton prison described him as "nauseating" and "sniveling" and he would whisper answers to questions he did not like; not unlike his demeanor during Evans' trial. He also allegedly dissociated when describing his actions, referring to himself in the third person; however, he boasted about his actions to other inmates saying that his "goal" was 12.

Trial, Conviction, and Execution

When faced with the myriad evidence against him, Christie quickly admitted to killing his first two victims but hesitated to take responsibility for Beryl Evans who he later admitted that he did, in fact, kill but not baby Geraldine. He said Beryl's was a mercy killing like his wife as a result of a botched suicide attempt on her part. Christie alleged that Beryl offered him sex to help her but he could not perform. None of the evidence corroborates Christie's account.

Christie's trial for murdering his wife commenced on 22 June 1953 at the Old Bailey. He pled not guilty by reason of insanity. His own attorney, Derek Curtis-Bennett, even called Christie a maniac and madman which was supported by Dr. Jack Abbott Hobson, a defense psychiatrist. The prosecutor's psychiatrists said that while Christie had a hysterical personality it was neurosis not a defect of reason and, therefore, Christie was not insane.

After a mere four-day trial and an 80-minute jury deliberation Christie was found guilty and sentenced to death. He did not appeal and was hanged at Pentonville Prison on 15 July 1953.

THE HILLSIDE STRANGLERS

NAOMI ROBERTS

Cousins Kenneth Bianchi and Angelo Buono, Jr. are collectively known by their media epithet "The Hillside Strangler". These two men were responsible for the murders of at least nine females, ages 12 to 28, during the late 1970s in Los Angeles, California, and Bianchi killed two more in Washington. After their first three victims did not gain much attention because they were prostitutes, Bianchi and Buono decided to abduct and murder middle-class "nice" girls. Five victims were found on hillsides in the Glendale-Highland Park area during Thanksgiving weekend in 1977 and the resulting panic led to the coining of the moniker "Hillside Strangler".

Lead Los Angeles Police Department homicide investigator Detective Sergeant Bob Grogan, along with his partner Dudley Varney as well as Los Angeles Sheriff's Department's Detective Frank Salerno, believed that the murders were the work of more than one killer but figured the less the murderers knew about what police knew the better.

Bianchi later moved to Washington where he murdered two more women before being caught.

Both Bianchi and Buono were convicted of multiple counts of first-degree murder and sentenced to life. Buono dies of a heart attack on 21 September 2002 while serving his time in Calipatria State Prison in Calipatria, California. Bianchi continues to serve his sentence at Washington State Penitentiary in Walla Walla.

Early Lives

Kenneth Bianchi

Kenneth Alessio Bianchi was born on 22 May 1951 in Rochester, New York, to a 17-year-old alcoholic prostitute who gave him up for adoption two weeks after he was born. He was adopted by Nicholas Bianchi and Frances Sciolono and despite a stable upbringing, Bianchi became a pathological liar at a very early age. Further, as a result of petit mal seizures he suffered at the age of five, Bianchi often daydreamt as if he were in a trance.

Bianchi suffered from insomnia and frequently wet the bed as a child (one of the triad symptoms of serial killers). Frances took him to the doctor on multiple occasions for his urination problem and being examined by the doctor caused Bianchi much embarrassment and humiliation. He also had a bad temper and was diagnosed with passive-aggressive personality disorder which is characterized by an individual who may appear to be enthusiastic about and actively comply with others' desires and needs while simultaneously resisting them, thus resulting in increased anger and hostility. At the core of this disorder is that the sufferer resents responsibility and instead of openly expressing his or her feelings, demonstrates said resentment through actions such as procrastination, forgetfulness, and inefficiency. Despite having a rather high IQ of 116, Bianchi was a chronic underachiever in school. When Frances took him to a psychologist, it was determined that Bianchi was overly dependent upon his mother.

On 2 January 1957, Bianchi fell off of a jungle gym and landed on his face. His mother then sent him to a private Catholic elementary school where he excelled in creative writing. In July 1963, Bianchi pulled down a six-year-old girl's pants after "spontaneously decid[ing] that he liked doing so".

His adoptive father died in 1964, thus leaving an unemotional Bianchi having to attend public high school where he joined a motorcycle club and dated frequently. His adoptive mother was forced to work and she was known for keeping Bianchi home from school for extended periods of time.

While in high school, Bianchi set high standards for his many girlfriends such as complete fidelity and outwardly absolute devotion; however, these standard did not apply to him.

He graduated in 1971 from Gates-Chili High School in Rochester and, soon after, married his high school sweetheart, Brenda Beck; however, the couple divorced after only eight months. Rumor has it that Brenda left without a word.

Bianchi enrolled at Monroe Community College to study police science and psychology after deciding that he wanted to become a police officer; however, after only one term he dropped out and then was rejected for several positions both in Rochester and, later, Los Angeles. Consequently, Bianchi worked a series of menial odd jobs, eventually becoming a jewelry store security guard for which he was fired for stealing and giving his girlfriends the stolen jewelry. He would steal from other employers over the years.

He then left Rochester and moved to Los Angeles in late 1975 at the age of 26.

Angelo Buono, Jr.

Angelo Anthony Buono, Jr. was born on 5 October 1934, also in Rochester, New York, to first-generation Italian-American immigrants originally from San Buono, Italy. His parents divorced when he was young and a five-year-old Buono moved to Glendale, California, with his mother Jenny and his sister Cecilia, where his mother supported the family by doing piecework in a shoe factory. Raised Catholic, this had no effect on Buono's development as a decent human being.

Buono displayed a very high interest in sex from a young age and when he was a teenager claimed that he had raped and sodomized number of girls. Buono idealized serial rapist Caryl Chessman, also known as "The Red Light Bandit", calling Chessman his hero but added that Chessman should have murdered his victims. He developed a deep loathing of women and desire to injure and humiliate them, including his mother who he would verbally abuse; however, he was emotionally tied to her until her death in 1978.

Buono began stealing cars and was sent to the Paso Robles School for Boys.

In 1955, Buono married his high-school sweetheart, Geraldine Vinal, who was 17 years old at the time, who he had impregnated; however, less than a week later he left her. She would later give birth to a son, Michael Lee Buono, on 10 January 1956. Buono filed for divorce and refused to pay child support or let his son call him "Dad". He was back in jail for car theft when his first son was born.

Later, he impregnated Mary Castillo who gave birth to his second son, Angelo Anthony Buono III, at the end of 1956 and then married her in 1957. The couple would have four more children: Peter in 1957, Danny in 1958, Louis in 1960, and Grace in 1962. In 1964, Buono was believed to have sexually assaulted his two-year-old daughter Grace; however, there is insufficient literature to know fully the circumstances of the allegation. Buono's second marriage to Castillo also ended in divorce that same year after she purported that he had been physically, emotionally, and sexually abusive toward her. In a last-ditch effort to reconcile with him, Castillo was "rewarded" with his handcuffing her and threatening to kill her at gunpoint. Castillo would later recount a night during the first year they were together where Buono tied her spread-eagled to the bedposts and "raped her so violently she was afraid that he was going to kill her" and "her pain seemed to him his greatest pleasure" and, thus, he had no qualms of hurting her and didn't seem to care that the children witnessed the abuse. He avoided paying child support again.

Buono married a third time in 1965 to a 25-year-old single mother named Nannette Campino and the couple had two children of their own: Tony in 1967 and Sam in 1969. Despite being treated as poorly as Mary Castillo had been, Campino feared for her life on a daily basis but stayed until he began to sexually abuse her 14-year-old daughter. Buono allegedly bragged that he raped his stepdaughter because "[s]he needs breaking in" and then turned her over to his sons for their pleasure. Campino finally took her children, filed for divorce, and fled the state in 1971.

Buono, again, was arrested for auto theft and was sentenced to one year in prison; however, due to his large family his sentence was suspended so he could work to support them.

Buono married yet again, on a whim, to a woman named Deborah Taylor; however, the couple did not live together, nor did they ever divorce.

In 1975, he became a car upholsterer and purchased his own place at 703 E. Colorado Street to live and work. Despite his abuse, cockiness, overbearing nature, and lack of good looks, Buono was considered very attractive by women, particularly younger ones who were usually naïve about sex so it was easy to convince them that his outrageous demands and proclivities were normal. Thus, he frequently forced women to engage in sex acts with him and began a relationship with a teenage girl whom he twice impregnated.

He was ugly inside and out; very coarse, vulgar, ignorant, selfish, and sadistic.

Bianchi and Buono Together

At the age of 41, Buono came into contact with his cousin Kenneth Bianchi, the latter who, in 1975, moved to California and in with his cousin. Bianchi found his older cousin with "dyed black hair, gold chains around his neck, a large gaudy turquoise ring on his finger, red silk underwear and a virtual harem of jailbait girls". Buono taught Bianchi how to use fake police badges in order to coerce free sex from prostitutes. When they needed money the two also became pimps for a short time until the two girls who worked for them—Sabra Hannan and Becky Spears—escaped after enduring relentless abuse by Buono. Bianchi, still desiring to become a police officer, applied for jobs at the Los Angeles Sheriff's and Glendale Police Departments but neither were hiring. He then procured employment with a title company and used his first paycheck on an apartment and a Cadillac, moving in with coworker Kelli Boyd. Boyd rejected his marriage proposal as she considered Bianchi to be very jealous, immature, and a liar; however, in May 1977 she told him she was expecting their first child together. The couple moved to an apartment at 1950 Tamarind Avenue in Hollywood.

Bianchi also rented some office space and set himself up as a psychologist with a fake degree and credentials. He did not have many clients and when Boyd found out she was outraged. During the "Hillside Strangler" investigation, Bianchi told Boyd he had lung cancer and was undergoing chemotherapy and radiation to explain for his work absences; however, this was a lie. One day, detectives came to his apartment to ask questions but were "favorably impressed" and did not consider him a suspect at that time.

The Murders

In October 1977, the two men committed their first murder together. Their M.O. was to cruise around Los Angeles and use fake badges to convince women that they were undercover police officers. After persuading them into Buono's car that the men said was an unmarked police car, the two would take their victims to Buono's house where they would rape, torture, and strangle them with their "signature" weapon—a garrote (a handheld ligature such as a chain, rope, or strap)—although some of their victims were reportedly killed by lethal injection, electric shock, and gas asphyxiation. Their bodies were thus disposed of outside, frequently in hilly areas.

Yolanda Washington, 19

19-year-old tall, leggy, African-American prostitute Yolanda Washington disappeared on 17 October 1977 from Cathedral City, California. She was found the next day dumped just outside Forest Lawn Cemetery, beaten, raped, and strangled with a piece of cloth. Her corpse was cleaned and there were faint marks around her wrists, ankles, and neck. Her body was posed in a grotesque sexual position.

Judith Lynn Miller, 15

On 31 October, 15-year-old Judith Lynn Miller, a runaway, was found in a La Crescenta-Montrose neighborhood, face up on a parkway in a residential area. The homeowner covered her with a tarp so that neighborhood children wouldn't see her. After the incident, that same homeowner relocated his family to another state.

The victim was small and thin, perhaps 90 pounds, with medium length reddish-brown hair. She had bruising around her neck. She had also been raped and sodomized and her body had been posed with her legs in a diamond-like position.

Los Angeles Sheriff's Department Sergeant Frank Salerno was called to the site. He noticed insect activity upon her skin and on her eyelid was "a small piece of light-colored fluff" that he saved for forensic experts. He surmised that she had been killed elsewhere and her body had been deliberately placed where it would quickly be found.

At her autopsy, the coroner determined that she had been killed around midnight and was raped and sodomized.

There was no missing person's report matching this latest victim so after a couple of days, Salerno had the newspapers run a small story on her with a request to contact the police if anyone could identify her. Still nothing. Salerno then took her picture to Hollywood Boulevard and showed it to hundreds of runaways, addicts, homeless people, and prostitutes. The name Judy Miller kept coming up as a young destitute prostitute. One man named Markust Camden—a self-proclaimed bounty hunter—told Salerno that he saw Judy Miller leave the local fish and chips restaurant at 9:00 p.m. the night before she was found dead. In fact, he would pick Buono out of a police photo lineup, but failed to recognize Bianchi.

Eventually, Salerno was able to track down the Miller family and got a positive identification. They had nothing useful to contribute to the investigation.

Elissa "Lissa" Teresa Kastin, 21

Lissa Kastin, 21, was working as a waitress at the Healthfaire Restaurant to pay for ballet lessons as she was an avid dancer. She also worked part time for her father's real estate and construction business. She was last seen leaving work the night of 5 November. She was found the next day near the Chevy Chase Country Club in Glendale on 6

November; which was also near to where Buono lived. She had been beaten, raped, and strangled to death.

Salerno compared notes with the Glendale Police Department and noticed similarities between his latest victim and this new one. Both bodies had the same five-point ligature marks—ankles, wrists, and neck—and had been dumped within six miles of each other. This latest victim had been raped but there was no evidence of sodomy.

When Salerno looked at the dump site he was confident that at least two men were involved due to the large guardrail between the street and where the body was found and the near impossibility that one man could have gotten her body over it alone.

Dolores Cepeda, 12 and Sonja Johnson, 14

After their early murders failed to attract much publicity, Bianchi and Buono decided to find some younger victims.

12-year-old Dolores Cepeda and 14-year-old Sonja Johnson were abducted in Highland Park, California, on 13 November. They had last been seen getting off a school bus heading home from St. Ignatius School and approaching a large two-tone sedan that, reportedly, had two men inside.

Both young girls were found on 20 November in the hills between Glendale and Eagle Rock, near Dodger Stadium by a young nine-year-old boy who was treasure hunting in the trash on the hillside.

Los Angeles Police Department Homicide Detective Dudley Varney had been called to this site.

Kristina Weckler, 20

That same day, 20-year-old Kristina Weckler was found on the other side of the same hillside where Cepeda and Johnson were found.

Weckler was a quiet, loving, and serious honors student at the Pasadena Art Center of Design and lived in Glendale.

She was found nude, raped, tortured, and strangled to death as evidenced by ligature marks on her neck, as well as around her wrists and ankles. She had blood oozing from her rectum and bruises on her breasts. Weckler was the first victim to show additional overt signs of torture; having been injected with Windex glass cleaner she had oozing injection marks on her arms.

Los Angeles Police Department Homicide Detective Sergeant Bob Grogan—Varney's partner—was called to this site. He noticed that there was no indication of any disturbance of the foliage in the area or evidence that the body had been dragged there. Grogan made a mental note that she likely had been killed elsewhere and then carried and dumped in this location by one or maybe two men.

At this point, police were entertaining the idea that there was more than one killer and that they were becoming increasingly more sadistic.

Jane Evelyn King, 28

28-year-old actress Jane King disappeared in Los Angeles around 10 November 1977, and was found near the Los Feliz off ramp of the Golden State Freeway on 23 November. She had been sodomized and strangled and her body was badly decomposed. After King was found, Los Angeles Police Department officials—in addition to Glendale Police Department and Los Angeles County Sheriff's Department officers—created a task force to catch the "Hillside Strangler".

Lauren Rae Wagner, 18

18-year-old student Lauren Wagner lived with her parents in the San Fernando Valley. Her parents had gone to bed on 28 November, expecting their daughter to return home before midnight. The next morning, they found her car parked across the street with the door ajar.

Wagner was found later that day in a wooded area near Glendale's Mount Washington area. She was lying partially in the street, nude, with ligature marks on her ankles, wrists, and neck. Wagner, too, had been tortured as the palms of her hands contained several burn marks.

At the dump site was also a "shiny track of some sticky liquid, which had attracted a convoy of ants". Police considered that if the substance was saliva or semen from the killer then, perhaps, his blood type could be determined, as tests on semen found inside the earlier victims revealed nothing. It was later found that Bianchi was not a secretor, in that his blood type could not be determined by other bodily fluids. DNA testing had not come into popularity at this time.

When Wagner's father questioned the neighbors, it turned out that the woman who lived in the house where his daughter's car was parked, Beulah Stofer, saw Wagner's abduction. Stofer said that Wagner had pulled over to the curb at around 9:00 p.m. and two men had parked their car beside hers. After some type of disagreement, Wagner "ended up in the car with the two men".

When Grogan went to talk to the neighbor, she told him that she had just had a phone call from a man with a New York accent who told her to "keep her mouth shut about what she had witnessed or he would kill her". Stofer also told Grogan that the car was a large dark sedan with a white top and that one of the men dragged Wagner from her car into his while Wagner protested, "You won't get away with this!" Stofer described one man as tall and young with acne scars while the other was older and shorter, Latin-looking, and with bushy hair. She said she was positive that she would identify them again. This statement rang true when she picked both Bianchi and Buono out of a photo lineup shown to her by Grogan.

Kimberly Diane Martin, 17

Tall, blonde prostitute Kimberly Martin, 17, disappeared from Echo Park, California, and was found strangled to death on 13 December 1977 on a steep hillside on Alvarado Street. Martin had worked for the Climax "modeling agency".

Police believed they had two reasonably good leads in this case. First, Martin's last "client" called her to 1950 Tamarind, apartment 114; however, this turned out to be a vacant apartment. Secondly, the murderer called from a payphone in the lobby of the Hollywood Public Library on Ivar Street. Unfortunately, nothing came from these leads.

Cindy Lee Hudspeth, 20

On 16 February 1978, 20-year-old Bible school teacher and secretary at an Echo Park church Cindy Hudspeth was found in the trunk of her bright orange 1977 Datsun B210 that had been pushed over a cliff on Angeles Crest in Los Angeles National Forest near La Canada. She had been raped and strangled, with the strangulation marks similar to those associated with the "Hillside Strangler".

Hudspeth was also a neighbor of Weckler even though the two women did not know each other. Interestingly, Bianchi also lived in the same apartment complex; however, this lead was never pursued even though both Grogan and Salerno believed that there was a good chance that at least one of the murderers lived in the Glendale area.

After this case, the lack of additional victims resulted in the disbanding of the "Hillside Strangler" Task Force.

Jill Barcomb, 18 (originally believed to be a Hillside Strangler victim)

18-year-old prostitute Jill Barcomb was abducted in Beverly Hills and found near the famous Hollywood sign on 9 November. Whereas it was originally believed that she was a victim of the "Hillside Strangler" because she had been raped, beaten, and strangled, in 2005, her death was conclusively proven through DNA analysis to have been committed by Rodney Alcala, the "Dating Game Killer".

Also, sometime in 1977, the two men gave Catharine Lorre a ride with the intent of killing her; however, when they learned that she was the daughter of famous actor Peter Lorre who played a child murderer in Fritz Lang's 1931 masterpiece film *M*, they let her go. She had no idea who the men were until they were arrested.

The two stopped killing after their ninth victim, Hudspeth (although at this time it was presumed they had ten victims with Barcomb), likely due to the birth of Bianchi's son and, as some surmise, that he had made some acquaintances within the Los Angeles Police Department who would take him on ride-alongs around the city, ironically, looking for the killers, and Bianchi could talk about nothing else while in police presence. On the night they had tried to abduct another victim, the two men got into a heated argument when Bianchi told his cousin that he had been questioned in the "Hillside Strangler" case. After Bianchi's confession about being questioned by police, Buono, furious, threatened to kill his cousin.

Bianchi's Washington Murders

Bianchi's girlfriend, Kelli Boyd gave birth to their son, Sean, in February 1978, and in March Boyd decided to return to her parents in Bellingham, Washington, as she was tired of both Los Angeles and Bianchi's lifestyle. After three months of pleading to be reunited, Boyd relented and Bianchi moved to Washington in May. Bianchi's role as boyfriend and father was relatively successful and he even took a job as a security guard, ultimately earning the trust of his supervisors. However, this way of life did little to alleviate Bianchi's murderous urges. Within six months he was actively looking for new victims.

On 11 January 1978, Bianchi lured two Western Washington University students—roommates Karen Mandic, 22, and Diane Wilder, 27—to a house he allegedly "guarded" under the pretense of housesitting. Once there, he raped, tortured, and murdered them.

On 12 January, police were informed that two female students were missing after Mandic's boss became worried that she didn't arrive at work that day. He did remember that she had told him she had accepted a housesitting job in a wealthy Bayside neighborhood from a security guard friend of hers. When former-priest-turned-Bellingham-Police-Chief Terry Mangan went to the girls' home he found a hungry cat, as well as the address of the home where they were to housesit. The name of one security guard kept coming up, as well as a record that Bianchi had used a company truck that same night, supposedly to take into the shop for repairs. This never happened. Mangan began to consider the fact that the women had met with foul play.

Police then went to the Bayside house and found a wet footprint. They also interviewed a neighbor who told them that a security guard asked her to check on the house except for the night the women disappeared because "there was special work being done to the alarm system and he didn't want her to be taken as an intruder".

After a press conference, a woman called police to report that a car had been abandoned near her home in a heavily-wooded area. In the car were the bodies of Mandic and Wilder. Both had bruising and had been strangled to death.

Mangan had the security guard picked up. He gave them no trouble. His name was Kenneth Bianchi.

There was ample forensic evidence in this case; most notably foreign pubic hairs on the girls and fibers from the house's carpet matching fibers on the dead girls' clothing and shoes. Additionally, when police searched Bianchi's home they found several items stolen from job sites where he worked.

Remembering back to the "Hillside Strangler" cases in Los Angeles—and knowing Bianchi had lived there—Mangan called the police departments in California who had worked on the task force. He spoke to Detective Frank Salerno to whom everything finally made sense. Detectives tirelessly worked to link Bianchi to the strangler cases and were confident that he was one of the murderers.

Investigation and Arrest

Bianchi was not as careful this time, having left significant clues, most notably his car with California license plates was seen and subsequently connected to the addresses of two Hillside Strangler victims. Without mastermind Buono, Bianchi didn't have the wherewithal to cover his tracks.

Bianchi was arrested the following day, on 12 January 1979.

Buono was arrested on 22 October 1979, after Bianchi told police about his cousin's complicity in the murders.

Trial and Conviction

Prior to his 1981 trial, Bianchi decided to plead not guilty by reason of insanity and claimed to have a separate personality named

"Steve Walker" who had committed the murders. After several interviews by experts specializing in multiple personality disorder and hypnosis, it was determined that he was faking. Immediately after Dr. Martin Orne mentioned to Bianchi that in genuine cases of multiple personality disorder there are typically at least three personalities, Bianchi created another alter ego named "Billy", shortly followed by two more. It was later determined that the name "Steven Walker" came from a student whose identity Bianchi had previously tried to steal to enable him to fraudulently practice psychology. Further, in Bianchi's apartment investigators found several psychology books which laid credence to Bianchi's ability to fake the disorder. He was eventually diagnosed with antisocial personality disorder with sexual sadism.

During trial, there was significant physical trace evidence against the two men; including fibers from Buono's upholstery from his home and workshop on two of the victims; an imprint of a fake police badge on his wallet; and hairs from rabbits he had raised on another victim.

Bianchi agreed to plead guilty and testify against his cousin in order to get leniency, albeit uncooperatively (evidence of his passive-aggressive personality disorder).

Judge Ronald M. George—who would later become California Supreme Court Chief Justice—said during Buono's sentencing hearing, "I would not have the slightest reluctance to impose the death penalty in this case were it within my power to do so. Ironically, although these two defendants utilized almost every form of legalized execution against their victims, the defendants have escaped any form of capital punishment." On an interesting side note, George's roommate at the time was author Darcy O'Brien who, four years after the trial, wrote a book about the case.

Both men were sentenced to life in prison.

While incarcerated, Buono married mother-of-three Christine Kizuka in 1986 while she was visiting her husband—and father of her children—who was in the cell next door to Buono at the Los Angeles

County Jail, serving 18 months for assault with a deadly weapon. She worked as a supervisor at the California State Employment Development Department.

Whereas the 64-year-old Bianchi continues to serve his life sentence at the Washington State Penitentiary in Walla Walla, Buono died of a heart attack on 21 September 2002 while serving life at Calipatria State Prison in Calipatria, California. Denied for parole on 18 August 2010, Bianchi will next be eligible for parole in 2025.

Aftermath

Bianchi is also a suspect in the "Alphabet Murders"—also known as the "Double Initial Murders"—which occurred in the early 1970s in his hometown of Rochester wherein three young girls were raped, strangled to death, and dumped in the wilderness. At the time he worked as an ice cream vendor situated near two of the murder sites. On 16 November 1971, ten-year-old Carmen Colon disappeared and was found two days later in Churchville, New York, 12 miles from where she was last seen. 11-year-old Wanda Walkowicz disappeared on 2 April 1973 and was found the next day in Webster, New York, off State Route 104, seven miles from Rochester. Finally, on 26 November 1973, Michelle Maenza, 11, disappeared and was found two days later in Macedon, New York, a mere 15 miles from Rochester. They were called the "Alphabet Murders" because not only did the young victims have the same initial for their first and last name but they were also found in cities which began with the same letter.

Whereas Bianchi has repeatedly tried to get his name cleared from these murders he remains a suspect because his vehicle was seen near two of the murder sites.

Another series of murders with similar circumstances occurred in California in the late 1970s and investigators have hypothesized that they are connected to the Rochester "Alphabet Murders". In 1977, Roxene Roggasch, Paula Parsons, and Carmen Colon (like one of the original "Alphabet Murder" victims) were found raped and dead.

Whereas Bianchi was tried for six murders, DNA exonerated him of the California "Alphabet Murders".

A 2008 movie entitled *The Alphabet Killer* was very loosely based upon the murders, and in 2010 a book written by Cheri Farnsworth called *Alphabet Killer: The True Story of the Double Initial Murders* was released.

In 1980, Bianchi started a relationship with a Veronica Lynn Compton, who was a defense witness during his trial. Compton, a cocaine addict who was fascinated by serial killers, was working as a scriptwriter in Hollywood. On one of her numerous visits with Bianchi while he was incarcerated, she gave him a copy of her screenplay entitled *The Mutilated Cutter*, about a female serial killer, and asked for this input. Compton grew increasingly fixated and allegedly fell in love with Bianchi. Later, she was convicted and incarcerated for attempting to strangle a cocktail waitress who she had lured to a hotel in a ploy to have the world—and authorities—believe that the real "Hillside Strangler" was still on the loose and that the wrong man was incarcerated. To make it look like an authentic "Hillside Strangler" murder, Bianchi manipulated and used Compton as a means to get out of prison by giving her semen of his smuggled out of the facility in a rubber glove to plant on the body. Despite that DNA forensics had not been utilized at that time, semen could still be analyzed to demonstrate the killer's blood type; however, Bianchi was not a secretor. The intended victim managed to get away and Compton was tried and convicted of first-degree attempted murder and sentenced to life. Compton was paroled from prison in 2003.

In 1992, Bianchi sued Catherine Yronwode for $8.5 million for putting an image of his face on a trading card. He claimed his face was his trademark. The case was dismissed with the judge saying that if Bianchi's face was, indeed, his trademark during the murders then he would not have tried to hide it from police.

In 2007, Buono's grandson, Christopher Buono, shot his grandmother—Mary Castillo who was married to Buono at one time—and then committed suicide. Christopher was unaware of his grandfather's true identity until 2005.

Bianchi and Buono are immortalized in film. The 1989 film *The Case of the Hillside Stranglers*—based on O'Brien's book—starred Dennis Farina as Buono and Billy Zane as Bianchi. In the 2004 film *The Hillside Strangler*, Buono was portrayed by actor Nicholas Turturro and Bianchi was portrayed by C. Thomas Howell.

The 2006 movie *Rampage: The Hillside Strangler Murders* starred Tomas Arana as Buono and Clifton Collins, Jr. as Bianchi.

In 2001 the Discovery Channel aired an episode of *The New Detectives* that revisited the murders.

Bianchi and Buono have also been mentioned several times on the television show *Criminal Minds* as an example of killer teams with psychopathic predatory sexual sadist personalities who murdered their victims together.

ROADSIDE STRANGLER

JASMINE GREY

When one envisions a serial killer, they think of a cold, calculating, heartless monster. As humans, some of us have developed ways to recognize other humans that are looking to cause us harm. If we look at a mug shot of famous another serial killer, like Charles Manson or Jeffery Dahmer, one could say that these men "look" like serial killers. Maybe it's because of their wild eyes, the way that they hold themselves, or the "creepy" feeling one receives from their presence. These factors are enough to make a person stay as far away from the killer as possible, but sadly, not all predators come with a warning sign. Michael Bruce Ross, later to be known as the Roadside Strangler, was a ruthless predator that slipped under the radars of the multiple women that he attacked, raped, and murdered. Detective Malchik, Ross' arresting officer, described this serial killer as, "There was nothing threatening about him, there was no signal to any of these people that there was a dark side or something that they should be afraid of. He was able to conceal that until it became time for him to attack these innocent, young women." Ross seemed to be an average-looking man of completely average-strength and abilities, but underneath his calm and normal exterior beat the heart of a man who struggled with his sadistic, sexual compulsions. When someone spoke to Michael Ross, they would say that he put off a very friendly and articulate demeanor seemed very well educated and kind, but it was merely a costume that he had created over a lifetime. The creepy part about Michael Ross, despite how honest and upfront he is about his murders, is the mystery behind his words. Is he being genuine or is this merely an act? Is he being honest or are we being deceived? His state of mind drifts from monotone claims to not possess any remorse for his monstrosities to genuine pleas for a chemical castration to reduce his perverse sexual desires. Michael Bruce Ross' case was a strange one, to say the least, and his mental condition will forever be remembered as a very dark part in Connecticut history.

The Childhood

Michael Bruce Ross was born on July 26, 1959. Among three other children, Michael Bruce Ross was born into the life of a middle-class chicken farmer. His mother Pat was impregnated in high school and forced into a shotgun marriage with Michael's father, Dan Ross. Needless to say, they did not go on to lead a very happy marriage. Pat Ross was a very mentally unstable woman, who underwent two abortions and was institutionalized twice. She abandoned her children and family once to run off with another man, but she soon returned to a depressing and emotionally unhealthy life on the farm. Pat Ross seemed to resent Michael more than the other children. His sister claimed that Michael received the brunt of their mother's aggression. Michael Ross claimed that he didn't remember his dark childhood or his emotional abuse-ridden family; he only had fond memories of working on his father's farm. The joyous memories of working on the farm centered on his peculiar job; Michael's job was to ring the necks of sick and malnourished chickens.

He recalled that he began to experience sexual fantasies around this time, like most boys his age, but they weren't anything like the hellish compulsions he faced in his adulthood. He explained his boyish daydreams as non-violent, although they might've been considered peculiar by most. In an interview, Michael describes his early, innocent fantasies of women, "I would kidnap women and take them to my safe place, and then they would fall in love with me, and never want to leave." It has been said that Michael was molested as a child by his mentally ill uncle while babysitting. As an adult, Michael Ross claimed that he did not remember this incident or his uncle at all; Michael was only six years old when the suspected uncle committed suicide. Whether Michael was too young to recall the incident or if he merely repressed the memory, the irreparable damage that comes along with molestation could be a very influential part of Michael's slip into sexual sadism. Despite his strange desires, his dysfunctional family, and his history of abuse, Michael was considered to be a pretty average child. As a teenager, he excelled in school, graduating as number sixteen in his high school class, and he eventually moved to Cornell University to study Agriculture and Life Sciences.

College Years

He continued to excel academically throughout his years at university. He studied Economics, Agriculture, and Life Sciences, and excelled in all of his academic endeavors. He joined the FFA (Future Farmers of America) and the Alpha Zeta fraternity. Ross' sophomore year roommate and Alpha Zeta brother, described Ross in 1977, "He kind of followed his own drum and went his own way." Michael never made any real connections in his fraternity, nor did he really make connections to anyone besides the long string of girls that he dated. In his college year, Michael Ross was rarely without a girlfriend, and he was rarely thinking about anything but. "There was always a certain obsession on his part regarding women," said his Alpha Zeta roommate, "That seemed to be such a big issue, a constant topic—needing a woman, needing to have a girlfriend. He would be obsessed about the relationship."

Ross claims that he did not experience truly violent sexual fantasies until his years at Cornell University. He especially did not begin to fantasize about raping women until his sophomore year in college. Michael Ross said that somewhere in his undergraduate years, he began to embrace the desires that brewed within him. He started his downward spiral with a very small step. He began to stalk his fellow students on campus. He would follow close by, making it known that he was behind her. "I would get a thrill by them knowing that I was following them. That they would be scared and that gave me a thrill," Michael explained his early experimentation with his predatory nature. When simply stalking the women wasn't enough, Michael eventually turned to towards rape. He hid in the bushes of Beebe Lake and raped a visiting student. Later, he attempted to rape another girl outside of the school observatory but failed. These assaults were only stepping stones to the full-fledged horror that Michael Ross was destined to cause. During his senior year at Cornell University, Michael Ross met Dzung Ngoc Tu, a Vietnamese student, and his very first murder victim.

The case of Dzung Ngoc Tu perplexed officials everywhere. She was found on May 17, 1981, in the Fall Creek Gorge. She died from a skull fracture and her body laid there for five days until she was discovered. It appeared to be a suicide, as if she had jumped from the bridge overhead and hit her head upon the fall, but there was no suicide note left at the scene. Close friends and family of Dzung Ngoc Tu claimed that there absolutely no signs of suicidal tendencies when she was alive and investigators found absolutely no reason for killing herself. Her body showed no signs of sexual abuse, there were no suspects, and the police had no idea that the culprit was actually Michael Ross, a man who was only connected to her by their similar majors. The case went cold when the police couldn't find a suspect. It wasn't until Michael Ross was already in prison for the murders and rapes of four other women when he confessed to murdering and raping a Vietnamese girl that went to his school in New York.

The Attacks and Murders of The Roadside Strangler

Michael Ross chose his victims merely off of chance and circumstance. If he encountered a woman that was in a vulnerable position, he felt this undeniable compulsion to attack. "There's nothing they could've said or done. It was me, it wasn't them," Michael Ross admitted with a solemn tone of voice, years after his final attack, "They were dead as soon as I saw them, I think."

Michael claimed that he only attacked women to relieve pressure that built up from his personal relationships with the women in his life. When he was working in North Carolina, shortly after he graduated from college, Michael recalled that he had a very difficult visit from his fiancé, which caused him to attack a random woman shortly after he dropped his fiancé off at the airport. He noticed a woman walking on the sidewalk with a baby stroller, so Michael pulled the car over and attacked her, using her own child as a weapon. "I told her that if she didn't do what I wanted, I would smash the baby's head against the wall of the house," Michael described in an interview, he seemed as if he were on the verge of tears, "I've always said that I never understood why these women never really resisted me. I'm not a big, strong guy, but nobody ever seemed to fight. I've always just contributed it as I must say something like that, or similar to it, to the other victims." He raped and strangled the woman, then left her for dead in her driveway.

On June 15, 1982, a 23-year-old woman named Debra Smith Taylor was attacked by Michael Ross in a park. He pulled her over where no one could see them, raped her, and forced her to roll over on her stomach; he then strangled her from behind. The young girl's body was discovered much later in a dried up river bed, only a few miles away from the location of another of Ross' victims, Tammy L. Williams. "Each time I killed, I made myself believe that I wasn't going to kill again," Michael Ross explained in an interview. It wasn't very long before he killed again.

His next attack occurred on a cold Thanksgiving Day in 1983. Michael Ross encountered Robin Stavinsky outside of Norwich State Hospital. He saw the woman in a vulnerable position and he took advantage of the situation. He forced the 19-year-old girl into a wooded area and demanded her to remove her clothing. Ross forced himself on the young girl then told her to roll over on her stomach. He strangled her from behind until the innocent Robin Stavinksky died in his hands. "Serial killers like to strangle their victims and that is, I guess, the most common form of killing because there's more of a connection there. It's more real and it's not as quick," Michael Ross explained why he enjoyed strangling so much. After he was finished with her, he covered her body with leaves and left her for dead.

The Roadside Strangler struck again on Easter Sunday, 1984. April Brunias and Leslie Shelly were hitchhiking on the side of the road when Michael Ross happened to drive their way. He pulled over and offered the young girls a ride. The girls did not find Ross threatening so they got into his car and asked him to drop them off at the next gas station. When Michael passed the gas station, one of the girls drew a kitchen knife and threatened to stab him. In an interview Michael Ross explained what happened next, "I almost drove off of the road, I was so surprised. I don't know what I said, but I said something and she gave the knife to me. It obviously scared her." He parked the car at Beach Pond and used a cloth to bound both of the girls by their hands and feet. He put Leslie Shelly in the trunk of his car, then dragged the girl named April a few feet away from the car. He raped the young girl, flipped her over onto her stomach, and strangled her until she died. He then took Leslie out of the trunk and did the same thing to her. "The smallest one, Leslie Shelly, has always bothered me more than the others. I think it was because she was so small, I think it was because she was so cooperative, and I think it was because the way she was killed was so close to the fantasy. That was the one that was... it was like it was fantasy," Michael explained. The girls were only fourteen years old when they were murdered.

It was a summer afternoon, around three o'clock on June 13, 1984, when the Roadside Strangler committed the murder that would finally get him caught. He was driving home from work when he passed Wendy Baribeault, who was walking down the side of busy Route 12 in Libson, only a few miles away from his home. Michael Ross pulled the car over and began to speak to this 17-year-old girl; he repeatedly invited her to his company picnic. After a little bit of conversation, Michael forced the beautiful, young girl over a stone wall and into the woods. "When I attacked her, I don't believe that I was in control. I don't think I would've been able to stop," Michael Ross explained his mental state during this attack, "I didn't really feel anything. I knew what was going on and I saw what was going on, but it was more like watching an old film..." Michael then raped the innocent girl and strangled her, just like the others, then entombed her in the stone wall that lined the busy road. The road was so busy, in fact, that there were several eyewitnesses to the attack.

The Investigation of the Roadside Strangler

The police had absolutely no leads on the murderer (a.k.a. The Roadside Strangler) that had taken Connecticut by storm. That was until Wendy Baribeault's body was found. There were dozens of eye witnesses to her attack and composite drawings were created that matched the facial features of local Michael Bruce Ross. Witnesses also noted that the attacker was driving a blue Toyota. Michael Malchik, the investigator assigned to the case, compiled a list of several thousand blue Toyotas. This tiny bit of evidence eventually led investigators directly to Ross' house, which was only three miles away from the location of the crime scene. Michael allegedly dropped hints that he was the murderer upon speaking to the police. "It all had to end," Michael Ross explained. It wasn't long before Michael was called into an interview with police in 1984. After a few hours of grueling interrogation, Michael Bruce Ross confessed to all crimes that he'd committed in Connecticut, but left out the murders in New York. "It's a mystery to me to this day, but it's typical of him," stated Detective Malchik, "Here he is, confessing to six murders, and he thought enough ahead not to tell us about the New York ones. Looking back at it, it's obvious he was thinking of something. He was always thinking two steps ahead. He's got his own agenda, but I couldn't for the life of me tell you what it is."

When Michael confessed to the murders, he seemed very sorrowful and remorseful, but he claimed not to feel a blink of remorse, "I don't want to say that I don't have any remorse, it's just like they weren't real..." Michael explains his feelings towards hid victims in a later interview, "I can't see them as I was killing them, so when I say I don't have any remorse, that doesn't mean that I don't have any regrets, or wish that didn't happen, or there was something that I could do to bring them back or anything – I don't have any feelings towards them. I feel like I should be tormented by them - by what they look like when I was killing them – or tormented by what was happening immediately before I killed them – but none of that's there. None of that's there at all."

"The only time he said he was sorry, was that he was sorry for getting caught," Michael's arresting officer explained, "He (Michael Ross) told me matter-of-factly, he said, 'If you hadn't caught me, I would've just kept on killing, again.'" This eerie statement by itself was enough to put the Roadside Strangler to death immediately, but his strange nature kept investigators questioning his motives behind being so upfront and honest about his heinous crimes. Did he secretly want to get caught? Was this all part of some big plot to instill his insanity?

Anne Cournoyer, Michael's correction counselor, described his mannerisms as he spoke of the horrible crimes that he committed, "One minute he's very, you know, looks like he on the verge of crying, and the next minute he's sort of giggling nervously - or sadistically – you just really don't know. You think that maybe, it's out of nervousness, but he could be getting pleasure out of talking about it."

A full-scale investigation of Michael Bruce Ross' life led to the realization of his wavering mental stability. Michael Ross explained that he could never recall the faces of his victims, even directly after the murders, "You'd think that if you killed someone, you would have the face imprinted in your mind and that you wouldn't be able to get it out of your mind – I don't have that. I never had that," He explained, "The only faces I could see was what was in the newspapers a few days later when they were missing. You know, the high school pictures and 'anybody know where this girl is?' type of thing. When I think of them, that's the picture that I see. I don't see them as they were when I killed them. If you had stopped me right after and gave me a composite drawing of like twelve pictures - you know - some blondes, brunettes, whatever – I wouldn't have been able to pick them out. Even immediately after I killed them."

The names of all eight women were: Dzung Ngoc Tu (25), Paula Perrera (16), Tammy Williams (17), Debra Smith Taylor (23), Robin

Stavinksy (19), April Brunias (14), Leslie Shelley (14), and Wendy Baribeault (17). He was only charged with the murders of the four Connecticut women because the murders of Dzung Ngoc Tu and Paula Perrera took place in New York. He was sentenced to death on July 6, 1987, but remained on death row for eighteen years after his sanity was called into question.

The Curious Case of Michael Bruce Ross

Michael spent the next eighteen years of his life caught in a battle of the Connecticut justice system. In court, a team of psychiatrists flocked to the defense of Mr. Michael Ross. After a parade of psychiatric evaluation, Michael was deemed mentally unwell, due to his dark childhood and his undeniable compulsions. Dr. Fred Berlin, the well-known co-founder of the Johns Hopkins Sexual Disorder Clinic, testified that Ross was struggling with a mental disorder called sexual sadism. Meaning that he gained sexual excitement from the pain and suffering of others. This discovery alone was not enough to save Ross' life, but Michael's claim to lose all self-control during the murders was enough to set back his execution date. Connecticut's state psychiatrist reluctantly agreed that Ross was not mentally capable enough to be responsible for his own actions, and therefore, it was not right to put him to death. Dr. Robert Miller wrote in a private letter, "I can't see how I could testify against psychopathology playing a sufficient role in defendant's behavior." Although this letter was never presented in court, Michael Ross' death sentence was overturned in 1994 and a new sentencing hearing was scheduled in 2000.

Michael Bruce Ross spent most of his time on death row writing about the mental disorder that took hold of his entire life. Michael claimed to have no control over his actions due to his compulsions. He described his sexual sadism as "a mental illness that drove me to rape and kill" and "made me physically unable to control my actions." During his time in prison, Michael still fell victim to his compulsions. It was impossible for him to control his sexual desires, so he spent the first few months of his incarceration reliving the murders. He claimed that he would fantasize these murders over and over again, hurting himself and causing sores from compulsive masturbation. It wasn't very long before he begged for some type of relief from his sexual desires, which came in the form of chemical castration. Ross was given medication that was designed to lower his testosterone levels and it finally relieved him from his sadistic compulsions. Thanks to this medication, Michael Bruce Ross was finally able to think clearly and he was able to see the true nature of his crimes.

The team of prosecutors naturally disagreed with the defense's attempts to lessen his blame. Prosecutors claimed that if he were unable to control his desires, he would've made less calculated attacks. It was reasonable to assume that Ross experienced these sexual desires constantly, which means that he probably experienced these feelings while in public places, or places where his actions could've been seen and reprimanded. Instead, Ross chose his victims very carefully, only acting when the girls were vulnerable and alone. Disproving the defenses' claims more so was the fact that Ross' hid their bodies after the attack, which further strengthened his blame and the case that he knew precisely what he was doing when he was doing it. "I'm not saying I wasn't there or it was multi-personality or any of that type of crap," Michael Ross later explained the strange fog he experienced while he murdered these innocent women, "I was there and I did it, but I wasn't one hundred percent there." To set light upon Mr. Michael Ross' guilt, Prosecutors relied on the "Policeman at the Elbow" test: would Ross have committed the crime even if a policeman had been standing next to him?

The defense team immediately disagreed with the statement that all of Ross' attacks were calculated and well thought out, considering the murder of Ms. Wendy B. who was murdered next to a busy road with several eyewitnesses, "When I attacked her, I don't believe I was in control. I don't think I could've stopped." Michael spoke about the murder that eventually resulted in his incarnation. "Could he control himself? Well, two juries rejected that," Detective Malchik recalls, "As the state's attorney said at the trial if Ross was so out of control, why didn't he just rape the girl in between the yellow lines of Route 12? He made it simple for the juries to understand."

John Blume, a professor at the Law school and co-founder of the Cornell Death Penalty Project, noted the how the jury in Ross' case did not take the opinions of the psychological experts seriously. "The thing that's disturbing," Professor Blume stated, "is that even when the experts all say your client is insane, juries will still reject it." Despite the team of psychologists on Ross' side, claiming that he was completely unable to stop himself from committing these monstrosities, the jury chose not to believe them.

Somewhere in the eighteen years of Michael Ross' incarceration, he decided that he did not deserve to live anymore. Shortly after Michael wrote a story called "It's Time for Me to Die", he reconnected with a woman named Kathy Jaeger, who served as his pastoral advocate that converted Ross to Catholicism. Ross wrote in a newsletter that Jaeger, "was able to breach my defenses and was able to touch my soul as no one else ever has." He later called Ms. Kathy Jaeger "the most important woman in my life" and claimed that "If I were a free man, I would ask her to marry me." Although Kathy rejects his claims to romance, she continued to support Michael Ross throughout his decisions.

After she entered Michael's life, there was a great shift in the nature of his case. Michael was done fighting for his life and the mental condition that wreaked havoc on his entire existence. After his original death sentence was overturned in 1994, the court ordered a new penalty hearing, but instead of going through the hearing with his public defenders, Ross acted as his own attorney. He worked with prosecutor C. Robert Satti to created what was deemed as "death pact" that allowed the imposition of the death penalty without a penalty hearing. "Please allow me to go into the courtroom . . . to accept the death penalty as punishment for my actions," Ross wrote in a letter to Satti. "I'm not asking you to do this for me, but for the families involved, who do not deserve to suffer further and who, in some small way, might gain a sense of peace of mind by these actions and my execution." The "death pact" was rejected by the judge as a "short cut" involving a human life, so Michael Ross flip-flopped back into his old ways. Ross returned to his defense team and reverted back into fighting for his life, claiming that his crimes were merely a product of his mental illness. He was resentenced to death soon after.

Jaeger said that Ross's sudden acceptance of death was a sincere attempt to provide closure for the families of his victims, "He told me, 'You know I don't want to do this. But I have to.' He just really felt anguish over what he had done. Really, really harsh anguish and self-loathing. Contrary to media reports, he doesn't want to die. He wishes that the justice system got it right years ago and gave him life sentences because he does have a mental illness. And the sad thing is, if they had done that, the families of his victims wouldn't have been re-victimized [by the ongoing appeals]. Michael is trying, in essence, to save them from any more of that."

Whether his acceptance of the death sentence was sincere, or not, Michael Bruce Ross was sentenced to death by lethal injection on May 13, 2005. He chose not to speak any last words before his death and died peacefully in the execution chair. Some family members believed that his death was too peaceful. Debbie Dupuis, Robin Stavinsky's sister, stated that she thought she would "feel closure" but instead just "felt anger" as she watched Ross simply lay there, go to sleep and die.

The state of Connecticut finally decided to end the life of the Roadside Strangler and put an end to the anguish that the families had to endure. After a very tragic and dark lifetime, Michael Bruce Ross and his sadistic compulsions were finally laid to rest.

Conclusion

Michael Bruce Ross is the type of cold, calculating, manipulative killer that we only read about in horror novels. His crimes almost seem too heartless and brutal to be true, but the victims of the Roadside Strangler would tell you that he is nothing but a cruel reality. In only a few years, Michael assaulted a countless number of women and murdered eight. Although he was only charged with four murders, Ross was forced to withstand eighteen long years of debate over his life sentence. In prison, he transitioned from a vicious killer who was truly non-remorseful for his brutal crimes to a man who seemed to genuinely regret his life choices and the pain that he subjected. Towards the end of his life, Ross begged for removal from his troubled existence, not only for himself but to end the long and grueling process of the legal system. Despite his transition into humanity, Michael Bruce Ross never took full blame for his actions. He flip-flopped between blaming his childhood, his compulsions, and his interpersonal relationships for these terrible crimes. He claimed to never feel any guilt or remorse for his actions, simply because he wasn't completely there while they were taking place. During these attacks, Michael claims that he was under some type of spell, some type of fog that completely disconnected him from his actions. He was completely able to murder and rape these innocent women without feeling guilt or remorse, or even being able to recall the very faces of his victims', only moments after their attack. Michael Ross was an extremely troubled man who suffered from a very extreme case of sexual sadism. Michael explained his cruel, heartless, attacks with vivid details and an undetached tone of voice. The scariest part about his calm demeanor is the monotone way that he described the way he stole the lives of these young, innocent women. He speaks as if he were not responsible for killing these beautiful and young women, although he willingly confesses to the murders. He claimed that he was merely a victim of his sexual compulsions since his college years and the women he attacked were merely in the wrong place at the wrong time. Whether his desires were really uncontrollable or if it was merely an excuse, Michael Bruce Ross' case remains to be one of the most perplexing cases in American history. His mere mental condition was enough to perplex the entire state of Connecticut – how could this well-spoken, articulate man with such a great personality, commit these terrible crimes? Why didn't anyone notice his decline and stop it? What was it that made this seemingly normal man snap into the Roadside Strangler? Although the answers to these questions are uncertain, they definitely are unnerving. Michael Ross was created by circumstances, by his dark upbringing, and a lifetime of people letting him slip through the cracks. Everyone saw him as an average, everyday college student, so no one thought to ask. The woman that he murdered were sadly only stepping stones into the downward spiral into his sickness and they were eventually caused the end of his vicious, murderous cycle.

STOCKWELL STRANGLER : The True Story of Kenneth Erskine

NATALIE MARSHALL

Kenneth Erskine, known as "The Stockwell Strangler" due to the geographic proximities of his murders, was a deeply troubled young man who had demonstrated worrisome signs of violence and schizophrenia from a young age. He was a gerontophile in that he had an unnatural sexual attraction to the elderly. Gerontophilia, essentially, is the opposite of pedophilia. Erskine would break into elderly men's and women's London flats and strangle them while they were in bed; after which he would rape and/or sodomize most of them. To demonstrate his own warped sense of love for his victims he would cross their arms across their chest, close their eyes, and tuck them into bed. Also, perhaps to hide his shame, he would turn his victims' family photographs face down. There was much speculation among mental health professionals that Erskine also suffered from schizophrenia from a very young age.

He was eventually convicted of seven murders and one attempted murder and sentenced to life in prison in 1988 at the age of 25. However, in July 2009, following an appeal his murder convictions were reduced to manslaughter on the grounds of diminished capacity and he received a hospital order to serve his life sentences at Broadmoor Hospital. While he has the potential to be granted parole in 2028, the trial judge's original order was that Erskine should spend at least 40 years behind bars, thus making him at least 65 years of age before potential eligibility for release.

Early Life

Kenneth Erskine was born in Hammersmith, London in July 1963. His mother Margaret was British and his father Charles was from Antigua. He was one of four boys, had an average IQ when tested at eight years old, and was remembered by neighbors to be a "chubby, Bible reading soul"; however, he became increasingly violent and difficult to control. For example, as a child, Erskine had tried to hang his younger brother, John, twice.

Erskine was then sent to a series of schools for maladjusted and troubled children where he received his formal education. He frequently and violently attacked his teachers and classmates and was identified as inhabiting a fantasy world with murderous impulses. In his own private fantasy world he would take on the role of Lawrence of Arabia, attacking and tying up smaller and weaker children—a theme that would resurface when he targeted the weaker elderly during his murder spree. During a school-sponsored swimming outing he had attempted to drown several classmates by holding their heads under the water until teachers were forced to intervene. He set fires at school and once pushed a classmate off of a moving bus. On another occasion he stabbed a teacher in the hand with a pair of scissors. In another event, a psychiatric nurse who tried to examine Erskine was taken hostage by him as he held a pair of scissors to her throat. He strangled the classroom guinea pig. Whenever any female staff tried to be empathetic and show him any type of affection he would expose his genitals or rub up against them.

There was frequent talk that Erskine demonstrated clear signs and symptoms of schizophrenia as a teenager but nothing ever came out of it. He never had therapy or medication or any real psychiatric evaluation.

By the time Erskine was 16 years of age he had turned to drugs and particularly enjoyed inhalants. This latest display of misbehavior was too much for his mother who eventually kicked him out of the house, forcing him to survive on his own. When Erskine tried to give his younger brother marijuana she finally disowned him. He never saw any of his family members ever again and was forced to spend the next seven years of his life "drifting through the twilight world of London's homeless and rootless" living in squats and hostels in Brixton and Stockwell and getting involved with petty crime which primarily took the shape of failed burglaries on primarily the elderly.

Erskine's violent tendencies continued to worsen.

When he was 18 he stabbed a young male with whom he was having a homosexual relationship at the time. Erskine had burst into his boyfriend's bedroom and stabbed and slashed at his body while he lay in bed. Whereas this may have been the first attack of someone in bed it was a glaring omen of the terror he would wreak in six years.

Erskine was described my many who knew him as a persistent loner who drifted through life and due to no direction of any type of social support system started a life of crime. Erskine was also a Rastafarian due to his Caribbean heritage but was shunned by fellow Rastafarians due to his habit of theft.

An unsuccessful burglar, he was jailed on many occasions.

Among Erskine's favorite "drugs" were solvents—such as glue—which he would inhale. Among the most oft-cited short term effects of huffing glue are hallucinations, delusions, and hostility. Long-term effects include depression, irritability, memory impairment, diminished intelligence, and serious and sometimes irreversible brain damage. There continues to be speculation as to whether Erskine was born with his psychopathic tendencies (nature) or whether his upbringing and environmental stimuli were to blame for his problems (nurture). The consensus is that a combination of factors worked together to create Erskine's sick and murderous persona.

Erskine subsequently spent considerable time in Borstals—youth detention centers—due to being apprehended following his many failed burglaries. While in one for burglary in 1982 Erskine would paint and draw pictures of elderly people in bed with gags in their mouths, with daggers in them, or burned to death. Additional pieces of "artwork" included headless figures with blood spurting out from their necks, people holding human hearts in their hands, disemboweled people, screaming faces, and copious pools of blood. Again, this was a chilling omen of what was to come. In one documentary about Kenneth Erskine and his crimes, one of his cellmates at Borstal, named James, described how horrific Erskine's paintings were and how he would frequently smile and laugh while painting them. As Erskine's only "friend" James became his confidant as well. The two would play chess to pass the time and then there were Erskine's disturbing paintings. James stated in an interview that Erskine always spoke very quietly—rarely above a whisper—and was very weird.

Borstal doctors were concerned enough to the point of asking the authorities not to ever free Erskine because they were seriously worried that he might try to replicate his paintings; however, he was, in fact, released and four years later he would begin his killing spree.

The Crimes

At some point Erskine decided to act out his fantasies and began to murder. He is classified as a geographically-stable serial killer who confined his murders to a specific area. As Erskine had no vehicle and roamed around the Stockwell area frequently confining his murders to this area was likely due to simple necessity.

The Stockwell section of South London is a favored place for the elderly to retire. In the summer of 1986, however, a serial killer conducted a reign of terror throughout the community that resulted in seven known deaths—and possibly another four—attributable to The Stockwell Strangler.

Eileen Nancy Emms, 78

Emms was a 78-year-old retired schoolteacher who lived in an "unkempt basement flat" on West Hill Road in Wandsworth. She was sexually assaulted and strangled by Erskine on 6 April 1986.

Emms' body was found on 9 April 1987 by her home help who, upon knocking on her bedroom door and receiving no response one morning, let herself in to find Emms in bed with the covers pulled up to her chin, seemingly asleep. There were no obvious marks upon her body. Initially, the cause of death was attributed to natural causes. The doctor called to the scene estimated that she died approximately three days earlier and signed a death certificate that stated natural causes.

Once the victim's home help noticed that her small portable television was missing, the police were called.

During her autopsy, the medical examiner revealed that Emms had been strangled by bare hands. There was heavy bruising to her chest which strongly suggested that her assailant had kneeled atop her while strangling her. Further examination revealed that she had been sodomized as the assailant had left semen around her anus.

A short Afro-Caribbean head hair was found on her sheet.

Janet Crockett, 67

Janet Crockett was Erskine's first July 1987 victim. She was chairwoman of her local tenant's association. Her body was found on 9 June in her flat in the Overton Estate in Stockwell. She had been strangled but, unlike Erskine's first victim—and subsequent ones—she was not sexually assaulted.

Police were able to immediately conclude that she had been murdered as she had considerable bruising on her chest due to sustaining two broken ribs as a result of someone kneeling on her while she was strangled to death. Additionally, her nightgown had been ripped from her body and folded neatly and placed upon a bedside chair.

Police also noticed that framed family photographs on the bedroom mantel had been placed face down or turned around. This action would be repeated at several of his crime scenes and speculation abounds as to what Erskine's underlying motive for doing this was. Some psychological experts have surmised that his anger at his own parents' rejection without a healthy outlet for his emotions led to an insane jealousy of normal family ties. Another hypothesis was that he felt ashamed at his actions and didn't want any "witnesses."

Police were able to find a smudged thumbprint on a displaced planter and a palm print on the bathroom window.

Pathologist Dr. Iain West conducted Crockett's autopsy and compared it to Emms. He concluded that their methods of strangulation were similar. He stated that with weaker elderly victims unconsciousness would occur within 30 second and death after approximately three minutes. While Crockett's and Emms' murders were similar—and that they were both elderly—police had nothing else to link the two victims.

Frederick Prentice, 73

In the early hours of 27 June, 73-year-old retired engineer Frederick Prentice was asleep in his council-run elderly people's home on Cedars Road in Clapham when he was awakened by the sounds of someone entering his bedroom. He saw a young man enter and Prentice turned on his bedside lamp and ordered the intruder to leave. Erskine then pounced atop the old man, placed his index finger to his own mouth as a threat for Prentice to be quiet, and then sat upon his chest where he alternated squeezing his windpipe powerfully, then relaxing his grip, and repeated this multiple times. Prentice told police that his assailant had whispered only one word over and over: "Kill." Prentice was able to push the alarm button near his bed which caused his assailant to leave.

After talking to Prentice the police were fairly confident that all of the victims thus far were, in fact, linked. A shoeprint found at the scene would also serve to connect this attack with some of the other murders.

Prentice would later identify Erskine in a lineup.

Valentine Gleim, 84, and Zbigniew Stabrawa, 94

The next day Erskine murdered 84-year-old World War II veteran Valentine Gleim and 94-year-old Polish immigrant Zbigniew Stabrawa in their adjoining rooms at Somerville Hastings House, an old folks' home on Stockwell Park Crescent. Both men had been manually strangled and sodomized.

The intruder had been seen by alert night duty staff but had vanished before the police arrived. Point of entry was, again, determined to be an open window. Staff were also able to see Erskine fleeing the scene and estimated his height at approximately five-feet-eight-inches with a slim frame so at least now investigators had a clue about their suspect.

Of particular concern in these two cases was the discovery of a used flannel towel and electric shaver which suggested that the murderer had calmly washed up and shaved after killing two people.

Approximately one hour prior to the double homicide an elderly woman in a Stockwell old folks' home was attacked while she was in bed by a man grabbing her arm. She fought off her assailant so vehemently that he had to run off. Her description of Erskine matched Prentice's.

William Carmen, 82

Two weeks after his previous double homicide, Erskine struck again by strangling and sexually assaulting 82-year-old widower William Carmen on 8 July. This time he threw a monkey wrench at detectives by murdering on the other side of the Thames river, in Islington, North London. Carmen was discovered dead in his bed in his flat on the Marques Estate by his daughter. As was the case with Erskine's other victims, Carmen was in bed with the covers pulled up neatly to his chin and had been sodomized.

This time there was clear evidence of ransacking and theft as approximately £400 of Carmen's savings was missing. Family photos were also placed face down or turned around.

William Downes, 74

On 20 July the body of 74-year-old William Downes was found by his son in his Holles House on Overton Road flat in Brixton; the same location where Erskine's second victim, Crockett, lived. He was naked and in bed with the covers pulled up to his chin, his eyes closed, and his arms folded across his chest—classic Erskine signature. Downes' son had reminded him to keep his windows locked firmly at night a few days ago so as not to fall victim to the Strangler but he failed to heed these instructions and point of entry was, again, determined to be through an unlocked window.

Downes had been strangled and sexually assaulted like the majority of Erskine's other victims. There were semen stains on the sheets.

Investigators lifted a palm print from the kitchen wall and another from the garden gate which were eventually matched to the prints found at Crockett's home. Finding the owner of these prints, however, was not as easy as the process is today. In 1986, while fingerprints were on file on computer discs at Scotland Yard, palm prints were not. Investigators had a stack of four million files; however, by concentrating on London-based burglars and petty thieves, they were able to compile a more workable load. They were subsequently able to match the prints to those Erskine, a small-time crook with an extensive rap sheet for burglary.

Unfortunately, the police did not know where to find Erskine and while they were looking he struck again, killing his final victim.

Florence Tisdall, 80

80-year-old partially blind and deaf Florence Tisdall was found in her apartment at Ranelagh Gardens near Putney Bridge on 24 July. The caretaker of the apartments noticed her walker in the communal corridor and knew something was wrong as Tisdall was unable to get around without it. He found her strangled, sexually assaulted, and with broken ribs as a result of her killer sitting atop her chest. She had spent the previous day watching the televised wedding of the Duke and Duchess of York—Prince Andrew and Sarah Ferguson—even having her own hair done especially for the big event. Tisdall had lived in an almost empty block of flats where she had resided for the past 60 years. A cat lady, she had left her windows open so the cats could come and go as they pleased and this is how Erskine got into her flat.

It was at this scene where Erskine made, perhaps, his biggest mistake. Detectives knew immediately that Tisdall had been murdered because she was found in her nightgown, tucked into bed with the covers up by her chin. In reality, however, Tisdall's neighbors who frequently checked on her because of her disabilities stated that she always slept atop the covers in the clothing she had been wearing that day. When Erskine undressed Tisdall to rape her, he attempted to cover up his misdeeds by making it look as though she went to bed as usual and died of natural causes. Family photos were also placed face down or turned around as was the case at the Crockett crime scene.

One of Tisdall's neighbors stated that she saw Erskine near the victim's flat shortly after the murder had occurred "looking disgusted with himself." Thinking this to be odd she promptly notified the police.

All of Erskine's victims were pensioners and in all but one case there was evidence of sexual assault that took the form of sodomy; however, investigators and forensic specialists cannot say whether it occurred before or after the victims' death.

Investigation and Arrest

After the Crockett murder, Scotland Yard's Serious Crimes Squad Detective Chief Superintendent Ken Thompson—a Scotsman with 26 years' experience—was put in charge of the case and given over 200 detectives to devote to the search for The Stockwell Strangler. Interestingly, Erskine was originally nicknamed "The Heatwave Killer" because the murders occurred during the summer; however, when the majority of his murders occurred in and around Stockwell this nickname was changed. Further, plainclothes officers would stand guard throughout the night wherever the elderly lived.

At the height of the investigation, as many as 350 law enforcement officers were on the Strangler case which included 150 detectives and senior officers from the C1 Murder Squad who worked out of five separate incident rooms throughout London which were linked to a special Home Office computer. This network was called HOLMUS and was used to prevent wasting time by cross checking paperwork which proved to be detrimental to the investigation for Peter Sutcliff, The Yorkshire Ripper. Other police officers set up fixed observation points in neighborhoods with a high population of elderly residents and instituted extra patrols.

A psychologist was enlisted to create a profile of the Strangler and to provide potential insight into his signature to determine whether he was attempting to cover his tracks or was fulfilling some bizarre fantasy. The suspect was determined to be suffering from gerontophilia; or a sexual attraction to the elderly and the complete opposite of its better known opposite, pedophilia. Speculation abounded as to whether the killer's sexual paraphilia was a result of some relationship problems with his grandparents. Additionally, as his victims were all selected at random, authorities could not link the victims together with the hopes of finding some commonality between them that would enable them to identify and apprehend the man responsible.

The suspect was classified as a process-focused serial killer. The majority of serial killers are of this type; the other being act-focused wherein their own psychological gratification from the kill itself is the underlying cause. Instead, process-focused killers achieve a hedonistic psychological "reward." These types frequently "get off" on the method of their kill and they enjoy the perverse sexual thrill that accompanies the act of killing. The literature identifies four types of process-focused serial killers: gain in which the killer kills for profit or personal gain; thrill in which the act of killing gives the killer a rush or a high; power in which the killer enjoys dominating and manipulating victims and while sex is usually involved it is primarily tertiary to the kill itself; and lust wherein murder is associated with sexual pleasure and this type of killer will commonly have sex while in the process or killing or may engage in necrophilia after death. As far as Erskine is concerned, he can be classified in multiple subtypes. First, since he did rob his victims and steal money he demonstrates some elements of the gain process-focused serial killer. Secondly, he did obtain a rush or high from killing his victims and, therefore, does demonstrate some elements of a thrill killer. This element is particularly salient when he was seen by a witness—who would later testify against him—getting sick on the sidewalk after his final kill near where his last victim was found. The act of his getting sick appears to be directly attributed to the thrill her received from killing and having sex with his victim. Finally, since Erskine likely sodomized his victims after he killed them his sexual fantasies were of a higher priority than is typically the case for power killers. Thus, he demonstrates elements more aligned with a lust killer.

Coupled with the fact that Erskine targeted the same type of people and that he engaged in specific rituals which were part of his signature makes Erskine a classic serial killer. His smaller size likely contributed to his choice of the elderly as his victims because in their weakened conditions he wouldn't have much trouble overpowering them.

The palm prints were the most damning evidence investigators had at that point; however, they only placed Erskine at two of the murder scenes. Despite similarities among all of the victims' crime scenes, the fact that Erskine wasn't cooperating with police required detectives to find other evidence. Investigators from Scotland Yard took the unusual step of distributing his Erskine's picture to the media to try to find more witnesses and potential leads by hopefully jog people's memories as to whether anyone may remember seeing him. Thompson also did something very uncommon; he appeared on television, appealing to Erskine to turn himself in.

After Tisdall's death the search for Erskine intensified even more than was already the case; however, being that he was a drifter with no permanent address or any real belongings to speak of they had to search through the hundreds of hostels and squats in South London. His life was so devoid of meaning and friends to help detectives find him.

Investigators got their big break when they realized that since the suspect was likely unemployed that he would be receiving social security and unemployment benefits. Upon further investigation they discovered that Erskine picked up his benefits on alternating Mondays from a Department of Health and Social Security office in Southwark, South London, and that he was due to collect his next check on 28 July. The building was placed under surveillance and when Erskine turned up, right on time, he was arrested and handcuffed without any struggle.

Whereas items and cash from the victims' homes were, in fact, missing, police did not believe that robbery was the driving motive in the homicides. There were neither signs of struggle nor any signs of forced entry. Police surmised that Erskine entered the flats through unsecured windows.

Forensic evidence linking the cases relied upon the fact that the victims were all murdered in similar ways: by the assailant kneeling on the victims' chests and then placing his left hand over their mouths and strangling them with his right hand. The semen collected at nearly all crime scenes suggested the same genetic fingerprint in that the same suspect was responsible for all of the sexual assaults. Additionally, there was a single hair found in Emms' flat, as well as matching shoeprints from three of the scenes.

A hairdresser informed investigators that Erskine had approached her wanting his head and pubic hair bleached. While she agreed to the former she refused the latter. Apparently, while he was sitting in the shop waiting for the bleach to take effect he self-applied the bleach to his pubic region and eyebrows, the latter resulting in his getting chemicals in his eyes and requiring assistance in washing it out.

When questioned by Detective Inspector Brian Jackson and other detectives, Erskine's responses indicated that the detectives' jobs were to be much more difficult than they thought. Erskine spent the majority of the interrogation giggling, staring out of the window or into the sky, or masturbating. After he was arrested, psychologists placed Erskine's mental age at 11 even though he was 24 at the time. He had first denied that he was, indeed, The Stockwell Strangler claiming instead to be a petty burglar who had no motive to kill anyone. After vehemently denying his culpability and blameworthiness in the string of murders and seeing that he wasn't getting anywhere, Erskine then changed his tune and said, "I don't remember killing anyone. I could have done it without knowing it. I am not sure if I did it." He also tried to blame the murders on a whispering female voice in his head. He once stated, "It tries to think for me. It says it will kill me if it gets me," and, "It blanks things from my mind."

He was clearly disturbed but not a fool in any sense. In fact, when searched, detectives found ten bank and building society accounts that Erskine had opened to hide the proceeds of his crimes. During the three-month span of murders, he had deposited over £3,000; quite a large sum of money for someone who was unemployed. This included a £350 deposit into one of his accounts on the morning after the Carmen murder. It was evident at this point that Erskine was amassing profits from his burglaries while simultaneously collecting unemployment benefits. This demonstrated that whereas Erskine did suffer from some degree of mental retardation and likely some psychosexual paraphilia he was not stupid by any means. In fact, he told detectives that his motive was to achieve notoriety. He said, "I wanted to be famous ... I thought I would never get caught."

During a lineup—or identity parade as it is called in England—surviving victim Frederick Prentice was able to definitively identify Erskine. Another woman who had witnessed Erskine vomiting on the sidewalk near Putney Bridge a mere 200 yards from the scene of the final murder on the night in question also picked Erskine out of a lineup.

Trial and Conviction

Erskine's trial commenced at the Old Bailey on 12 January 1988. He pled not guilty to the charges of seven murders and the attempted murder of Prentice. During his trial he would stare out the window or down at his feet as was the case when he was interrogated. When details of the murders were brought up, Erskine would masturbate.

The jury heard him confess to the burglaries of the deceased victims; however, he claimed that someone else must have followed him and killed the individuals after he had left. Nobody was buying this story.

After an 18-day trial, the jury unanimously found him guilty on all eight counts and he was sentenced to seven life terms plus 12 years for attempted murder with a recommended minimum of 40 years; one of the heaviest penalties ever handed out in British legal history. However, diagnosis of schizophrenia and other mental illnesses pursuant to the Mental Health Act of 1983 led to a successful appeal of Erskine's murder charges which were eventually reduced to manslaughter. He is currently serving his time at the Broadmoor Hospital.

In addition to his seven known victims, the police suspected Erskine of four other murders for which he has never been charged due to insufficient evidence to prove that he was, in fact, the murderer.

John Jordan, 57

On 4 February 1986, 57-year-old John Jordan was found in his Josephine Avenue flat in Brixton strangled beside his bed.

Charles Quarrell, 73

73-year-old Charles Quarrell was found suffocated in his bed on King James Street in Suffolk on 6 May. He had two handkerchiefs stuffed into the back of his throat, effectively blocking his windpipe.

Wilfred Parkes, 70

70-year-old Wilfred Parkes was found on 28 May in his Stockwell flat, suffocated and in bed. A nearby pillow was presumed to have been the murder weapon.

Trevor Thomas, 75

On 12 July 75-year-old Trevor Thomas was found dead in the bath at his home on Barton Court, Clapham. As Thomas had been dead for quite a while there was inadequate forensic evidence for investigators to link his murder to the others; thus resulting in Erskine not being charged with his death even though Thomas was almost certainly one of his victims.

As mentioned, Erskine has never been charged with these additional deaths; however, police were so confident that Erskine murdered them that they effectively closed the book on all of these cases. There is also much speculation that he likely killed prior to his first known victim—such as was the case with Mr. Jordan—and that because of his choice of victims their deaths may have simply been attributed to natural causes.

Aftermath

There is not much more information on Erskine due to a lack of any detailed studies of him as is commonly the case with other serial killers where the literature is rife with speculation as to what influences led to the individual turning to serial murder. His only possessions were meager clothes and some books from the building society. Other than a post-arrest diagnosis of schizophrenia, the mind of Kenneth Erskine remains mostly shrouded in mystery. In fact, his mentally-disturbed state has worsened to the point where he has been told that he will never be released from Broadmoor Hospital.

Psychiatrists have never been able to fully penetrate his mind and discover what makes him tick. He clearly has a problem differentiating fantasy from reality and appears to be locked in his own childlike world. However, there is one incident that clearly demonstrates his understanding between right and wrong. On 23 February 1996, Erskine prevented the possible murder of Peter Sutcliffe, known as the "Yorkshire Ripper" by alerting guards while another inmate, Paul Wilson, attempted to strangle Sutcliffe with the flexible cord from a pair of stereo headphones. Erskine was able to restrain Wilson from inflicting further injury upon Sutcliffe until guards arrived.

Erskine found himself on the receiving end of an assault. On Christmas Eve in 1997 he was attacked by fellow inmate, 34-year-old

Keith Hanger. Hanger was serving time for the 1992 shooting of his friend after having escaped from prison. He walked up to Erskine and squirted liquid from an aerosol can into his face before lighting it with a lighter. Erskine was taken to Frimley Park Hospital in Surrey, in agonizing pain and worried that he would lose his eyesight; however, his temporary blindness was just that—temporary.

Psychiatrists continue to attempt to probe Erskine's mind trying to uncover more and more of his psyche toward, perhaps, finding what makes him tick. Currently, he is unable to answer for his crimes, as demonstrated by the reduced sentence due to diminished capacity.